DEMOCRACY AND DYSFUNCTION

DEMOCRACY AND DYSFUNCTION

SANFORD LEVINSON

JACK M. BALKIN

The University of Chicago Press   *Chicago and London*

The University of Chicago Press, Chicago 60637
The University of Chicago Press, Ltd., London
© 2019 by The University of Chicago
For more information, contact the University of Chicago Press,
1427 E. 60th St., Chicago, IL 60637.
Published 2019

28 27 26 25 24 23 22 21 20 19   1 2 3 4 5

ISBN-13: 978-0-226-61199-0 (cloth)
ISBN-13: 978-0-226-61204-1 (paper)
ISBN-13: 978-0-226-61218-8 (e-book)
DOI: https://doi.org/10.7208/chicago/9780226612188.001.0001

Library of Congress Cataloging-in-Publication Data
Names: Levinson, Sanford, 1941– author. | Balkin, J. M., author.
Title: Democracy and dysfunction / Sanford Levinson, Jack M. Balkin.
Description: Chicago; London: The University of Chicago Press, 2019. |
Essays on whether the United States is in a constitutional crisis and
what can be done if it is, taking the form of an epistolary
exchange between two constitutional law scholars. |
Includes bibliographical references and index.
Identifiers: LCCN 2018050984 | ISBN 9780226611990 (cloth: alk. paper) |
ISBN 9780226612041 (pbk: alk. paper) | ISBN 9780226612188 (e-book)
Subjects: LCSH: Constitutional law—United States. | Democracy—
United States. | United States—Politics and government—2017–
Classification: LCC KF4552 .L483 2019 | DDC 342.73—dc23
LC record available at https://lccn.loc.gov/2018050984

♾ This paper meets the requirements of ANSI/NISO Z39.48-1992
(Permanence of Paper).

To Mark Graber
Hoping for peace—and for justice

To Stephen Griffin
Hoping for the restoration of trust

CONTENTS

INTRODUCTION

This book began with an invitation for the two of us to speak about the current problems of constitutional dysfunction in the United States at a conference sponsored by the Indiana University Robert H. McKinney School of Law in Indianapolis, held on November 6, 2015, and entitled "Partisan Conflict, Political Structure, and Culture."

We have been friends and coauthors for many years, and over the course of our collaboration, we have edited two books and written over twenty articles together. We still disagree about a few issues, however, and one of them is constitutional reform. Rather than prepare two separate essays, we decided to continue our collaboration in a somewhat different form—an epistolary exchange, which would allow us to explore each other's positions and what we consider their strengths and weaknesses.

Levinson has now written two books, *Our Undemocratic Constitution* (2006) and *Framed: America's 51 Constitutions and the Crisis of Governance* (2012), arguing that the American Constitution is outmoded and undemocratic—and that Americans should take up the example of the Founding Fathers. They should hold a new constitutional convention or, at the very least, adopt a series of new constitutional amendments. Although he does not reject the relevance of political culture, demographics, and contemporary media in explaining our present discontents, he believes that we ignore the implications of basic constitutional structures at our peril.

In his 2011 book *Living Originalism*, Balkin has argued that most constitutional change in American history—especially from the twentieth century onward—has occurred outside of the amendment provisions of Article V. The Constitution-in-practice—the constitutional system of government as we understand it today—changes as political regimes rise and fall and as successive waves of social mobilization and counter-mobilization push for reforms through legislation, institution building, political convention, and judicial interpretation.

We therefore have decidedly different views about the causes and cures of political dysfunction in the United States. Levinson emphasizes that much of our present-day political dysfunction can be traced to the text of the Constitution itself. Its structural provisions—many of which were undemocratic from the start and designed to make difficult the passage of new legislation that might challenge the status quo—have eventually caused politics to grind down into a biased, gridlocked, and unworkable system of government. The remedy is a series of new constitutional amendments or a new constitutional convention, rather than trying to persuade judges to interpret the Constitution in innovative ways.

Balkin, on the other hand, argues that the problem is best described as a problem of democratic representation, not dysfunction. Our political system has become undemocratic—because it no longer responds to popular will—and it has become unrepublican (with a small "r") because it is not fairly representative, allows too much self-entrenching behavior, is deeply corrupt, and is not directed at the achievement of the public good. America has become, in short, an oligarchy. Dysfunction is a different matter: the federal government appears dysfunctional because the old Reagan regime is breaking down and we are in a slow and agonizing transition to a new political regime, one that will probably be led by the Democratic Party or its successor. That transition will occur without the need for either a constitutional amendment or a new constitutional convention. The problem of oligarchy is far more important.

The Indiana conference offered a perfect platform for airing our contrasting views. We continued our correspondence for many months after our initial presentations, and the resulting letters were published in the *Indiana Law Review* in December 2016. But events continued to amaze, and we decided to continue our exchanges, both for our own edification and for the potential readers of a book on constitutional reform that we began envisioning—and that you now hold in your hand.

When we began our correspondence in the fall of 2015, each of us assumed that Hillary Clinton would win the Democratic nomination for president and most likely the presidency as well. Because of the extreme polarization of contemporary politics, however, significant legislative reform now requires that the same political party win the trifecta of the White House and both houses of Congress. If Clinton won, this seemed very unlikely, not least because of the relentless (and effective) Republican gerrymanders of the House of Representatives following the 2010 census.

We therefore expected that Clinton's election—coupled with Republican majorities in one or both houses of Congress—would lead to four years of further dysfunction and political trench warfare between the two major political parties. There would be endless investigative hearings by a Republican-controlled House or Senate (or both). There was even the outside possibility that Republicans, if politically daring enough, might try to impeach the second President Clinton just as they had the first. All this, we expected, would be grist for the mill of our debate on the nature and causes of dysfunction in American politics. It is also fair to say that although Donald Trump soon dominated the country's political attention, we thought it very unlikely that he would actually win the presidency.

We were wrong.

Instead, in probably the greatest upset in American presidential history, Donald Trump defeated Clinton in the Electoral College. (She won the popular vote by approximately 3 million.) Trump's victory, and its meaning for American democracy, put our previous analyses of the causes of American political dysfunction in a different and especially troubling light. It led to yet more letters to each other. We made the decision to conclude our epistolary exchange at the end of 2017, a year after Trump's election and nearly a year into his presidency. Obviously, these letters could continue indefinitely, but we believe that readers might benefit from seeing how two theorists of the American Constitution understood (and perhaps misunderstood) what was happening in the period between October 2015 and the beginning of 2018.

We have tried, as much as possible, to keep the letters in their original form, so that the reader can witness the evolution of our thinking as we and the rest of the country traveled through the convulsions of the 2016 election and Trump's first year in office. Nevertheless, we have added a few updates in brackets (this book went to press in the summer of 2018). We have also provided a very few explanatory footnotes for sources quoted and used. However, in order to preserve the informality of a correspondence between friends, we have tried to keep these footnotes to a minimum and instead offer a bibliography at the end. Readers who want full citations for at least the early letters can read the version published in the *Indiana Law Review*, which conforms to the American law review convention that every statement be fully documented.[1]

Throughout these letters, we try to understand the trajectory of events, where they have come from, and where they are going. Our predictions are by no means perfect—after all, neither of us expected that Trump would win! And, as the letters reveal, our thinking evolved as we lived through this explosive period. Our final letters sum up what we think we have learned in the process. Perhaps most important, each of us believes that the election of Trump is a symptom of deeper causes, and our arguments aim at uncovering those causes in constitutional culture and constitutional design.

Because our focus is larger than Trump's presidency, we hope—and believe—that how we analyze the current moment will be valuable to readers long after the events discussed in this book have passed. Even if we are mistaken, these letters give a sense of what it was like for two constitutional scholars to encounter an almost totally unexpected turn of events in American politics.

The questions of how and why our Constitution works, and how and why it needs to change, run deeper than our specific views about 2015–2017. In the best of all worlds, our mutual concerns about the fate of our country—and the world in which it plays such an important role—will prove to be exaggerated. We hope that the nation will quickly recover from the consequences of the 2016 election and the Trump presidency. But neither of us is Panglossian, and we fear that Americans—and the world—will be living with those consequences for a long time to come. We therefore hope that people reading these letters years from now will continue to find something valuable in them—not least, how to understand the constitutional dysfunctions

---

1. Sanford Levinson and Jack M. Balkin, "Democracy and Dysfunction: An Exchange," *Indiana Law Review* 50 (2016): 281.

of their own time, as well as the rise of the next demagogue who will seek to beguile the American public.

Sanford Levinson
Jack Balkin
Austin, Texas, and New Haven, Connecticut, June 2018

PART ONE

DO WE HAVE A DYSFUNCTIONAL CONSTITUTION?

SEPTEMBER 29, 2015

Dear Jack,

It is obviously no longer controversial that the American political system, especially at the national level, is seriously dysfunctional. In a recent essay, "Anxieties of Democracy," the distinguished Columbia political scientist and historian Ira Katznelson has remarked on the ironic contrast between recent repairs to the United States Capitol building and the continuing decay of the political institutions inside that same building: Physical "restoration is underway, its conclusion in sight. Inside, however, repair seems a long way off, if it is even possible." Katznelson continues:

> The House and Senate are presently shackled. Paralyzed by party divisions, influenced excessively by moneyed interests, and perverted by the disappearance of civic virtue, representative institutions appear unable to identify and address our most consequential public problems, including the politics of redistribution, racial equity, immigration, and the proper balance between liberty and national security. Like the dome, American democracy badly needs reconstruction.

Depending on one's place along the political spectrum, one might identify different examples of the particular failings of Congress, the presidency, and the judiciary. Those on the right are presumably less upset than those on the left that Congress's only apparent interest in redistribution has been to take from the less well-off and give to the wealthy via tax cuts and subsidies. As I write this opening missive, on September 28, 2015, RealClearPolitics, aggregating a number of recent polls, indicates that while approximately 15 percent of the public "approve" of Congress, 75 percent do not. The "direction of country" data indicates that only very slightly more than a quarter of polled Americans believe the country is heading in the right direction, while 63 percent (including yours truly) believe we continue on a downward slope.[1]

Katznelson offers a fairly familiar litany of examples of what "shackle[s]" our present system, including political polarization, the obscene role played by money in the overall electoral process, and, interestingly enough, "the disappearance of civic virtue." With regard to the last of these, one can well wonder exactly when a sufficient supply of such virtue in fact graced our political order.

One can scarcely understand the Publian argument for adoption of the Constitution as resting on a robust confidence in the virtue of the populace at large. Were that the case, one might have expected something other than the exclusive reliance on representatives and the absolute shackling of the public with regard to any direct participation in governance. There is a reason, after all, that in *Federalist* No. 63 Publius takes great pride in, and indeed emphasizes, what he regards as one of the strongest features of the new constitutional order: "THE TOTAL EXCLUSION OF THE PEOPLE, IN THEIR COLLECTIVE CAPACITY" from any share in actual governance. Decisions are to be made only by those deemed, with whatever empirical accuracy, the "representatives" of the people.

Publius assumed that these representatives would in fact be markedly "better" than their constituents. They not only would be more sophisticated about the ways of the world, but also, and more importantly, more disposed to tame the inevitable and ineradicable urges of self-interest, delineated most sharply in *Federalist* No. 10, and to be guided instead by the demands of the public good.

That vision of "enlightened" representation seems far in the past; the only serious debates today are whether the Publian vision ever made much sense and when it collapsed, perhaps with the emergence of the first party system around 1796, the rise of mass political parties

---

1. RealClearPolitics (www.realclearpolitics.com) offers the latest polling data on this question.

during the Jacksonian era, or the rise of the modern mass—and then social—media society in the twentieth and twenty-first centuries. (You certainly know far more about this last than I do, and, of course, much of your previous work also emphasized the crucial role of social movements in understanding the actualities of American constitutional development.)

As you no doubt can predict, given our many conversations (and joint seminars) on the general subject of the state of American politics, what upsets me about Katznelson's analysis—and, for that matter, the responses offered by a variety of talented academics and social activists—is that none of them, save perhaps for Hélène Landemore, comes close to addressing the possibility that among the cause of our present discontents is the institutional order created in 1787 and left remarkably unchanged since then.

It is especially telling that this failure of imagination is found in a symposium that is dominated by people on the left. They are, after all, fully aware of the deficiencies of our present political system and believe that reform—generally of the kind that I presume both of us would favor—is necessary. There was a time, however, when leftish critics were also at the same time critics of the Constitution itself. Perhaps they accepted, rightly or wrongly, historian Charles Beard's understanding that our Constitution was intended to—and did— serve the economic interests of the wealthy and powerful, rather than the working class (or, even more certainly, that subset of the working class called slaves). But those criticisms were not limited to particular judicial decisions—they also concerned constitutional design.

Take, for example, the totally unjustifiable power given small, usually rural, states in the Senate. It is surely no coincidence that Socialist Representative Victor Berger, representing Milwaukee early in the twentieth century, believed that the best reform of the Senate was not the popular election of senators, achieved via the Seventeenth Amendment in 1913, but rather the out-and-out abolition of that egregious institution. And in 1912 Teddy Roosevelt campaigned for the right of the American electorate to overturn offensive judicial decisions by popular referendum. (This was, of course, the historical period during which many western states, including, most notably, California, chose to supplement "representative democracy" with the "direct democracy" of the initiative and referendum.)

My point is that the agenda of political reformers once included "constitutional reform" in a sense far different from supplicating judges for attractive decisions. That approach to constitutional reform has been lost, save, interestingly enough, for certain members of the Tea Party who, for example, would like to repeal the Seventeenth Amendment (not to mention the Sixteenth Amendment's authorization of the federal income tax).

That spirit of constitutional reformism seems completely absent in the contemporary left, including that portion of the left represented (or, some would say, over-represented) in the legal academy. In 2009, for example, you and our mutual friend Reva Siegel coedited a book on constitutional reform for the American Constitution Society (ACS) (which I am glad to support), entitled *The Constitution in 2020*. My principal objection to the book was that it was devoted exclusively to judicially managed reform. It had no discussion at all about whether the members of the ACS should seek something that judges cannot in fact provide—fundamental institutional change.

As you know, I have written a series of books explaining the many defects in our Constitution. I believe that law professors spend too much time debating changes in constitutional doctrines—what I call the "Constitution of Conversation." The real problems, I believe, rest in the parts of the Constitution that few people—including law professors—ever talk about. These are the structural features that I call the "Constitution of Settlement."

My third book on the defects of our Constitution—coauthored with my wife, Cynthia, and directed primarily at teenagers—is entitled *Fault Lines in the Constitution*. So let me set out some of the primary fault lines or hidden dangers in the Constitution of Settlement.

First, we have no way to get rid of an unfit or dangerously incompetent president except through the unwieldy method of impeachment and removal or, even more unlikely, the Twenty-Fifth Amendment. We would be far better served if Congress could remove the president by a vote of no confidence—a procedure available in many parliamentary systems. As it is, the fixed presidential term of four years, coupled with our obviously ineffective procedures for impeachment or the Twenty-Fifth Amendment, condemns us to the continued rule of individuals who lack the capacity to handle fundamental issues of war and peace—and of life and death.

Second, it is far too difficult to pass necessary reforms through Congress. Our legislative process is effectively "tricameral" because of the president's veto power. Add to this a wide range of other veto points in our legislative system that make it extremely difficult for the national government to pass legislation that is, in the language of the Constitution, "necessary and proper" to achieve the great aims set out by the Preamble, including "establishing justice" and "providing for the general welfare."

Third, perhaps the worst feature of our legislative process is the organization of the Senate, in which each state receives two votes. This arrangement is almost self-evidently illegitimate under the constitutional principle of "one person, one vote." Each American deserves equal representation in our government. As Justice John Marshall Harlan put it in his famous dissent in *Plessy v. Ferguson*, there is no special class or caste of citizens in the United States. But our malapportioned Senate makes a mockery of that worthy goal, giving people in tiny states like Wyoming and North Dakota many times the voting power and influence of people living in states like Texas or California. To give you a sense of the severe imbalance: Nine states together now contain more than a majority of Americans, yet they are represented by only eighteen senators. By contrast, less than one-half of the population—who live in forty-one states—receive a grand total of eighty-two senators. This severe malapportionment has wide-ranging effects in the kinds of interests that Congress serves and the kinds of reforms that Congress is able to pass, causing immense frustration and a sense that government is unaccountable to the public.

Fourth, our constitutional system for choosing presidents, the Electoral College, is nothing short of a scandal. It puts people in the Oval Office who do not even come in first in the popular vote. [This has now happened twice in sixteen years—in 2000 and 2016, giving us George W. Bush and Donald Trump.] Moreover, even when a candidate receives a plurality, like Richard Nixon in 1968 and Bill Clinton in 1992, the "first past the post" winners may fall far short of a majority. Both Nixon and Clinton received only 43 percent of the popular vote and could scarcely claim a genuine "mandate" for their policies.

Fifth, our process of constitutional amendment is extraordinarily difficult. This makes it nearly impossible to engage in serious constitutional reform—the most important episode of such reform required a war that killed 750,000 Americans—and it also serves to discourage any serious discussion of such reform precisely because it appears to be futile. As I've written elsewhere, the operative mantra is not "If it isn't broken, it doesn't need fixing," but, instead, "Because it cannot, as a practical matter, be fixed, let's pretend it isn't broken."

All of these features of the Constitution, and others as well, taken together, form the basis of what my first book called "our undemocratic Constitution." Perhaps more important, these defects of our constitutional system help to explain what the subtitle of my second book, *Framed*, called our "crisis of governance." An important symptom of that crisis of governance is the loss of public esteem not only for Congress (which is well deserved), but for all national institutions other than the military.

Let me stop now. I trust I have said enough to initiate this epistolary exchange. With regard to grasping the causes for our dysfunctionality, there is much to be said for the importance of American political culture; as Mark Graber has sometimes suggested, we may need new kinds of citizens rather than a new Constitution. Similarly, partisan conflict of the kind analyzed by, say, Norman Ornstein and Thomas Mann is surely worth a great deal of emphasis. But I hope that "political structure" does not get lost in the conversation. Are we well served by the set of structures created in 1787, and could we do better? I believe that the answer to the first question is clearly no, and I am agnostic about the possibility of doing better. But we will never know unless we begin a full-scale conversation about what institutional transformation might actually involve. The absence of that conversation is one of the glaring deficiencies in our collective discussions of the health of the American polity. I do not think it is the *only* thing we need to talk about, but I do strongly believe that any approach that denies its potential importance is doomed to failure.

I look forward to reading your reply.

Sandy

OCTOBER 12, 2015

Dear Sandy,

It might be useful to organize the issues raised by your initial comments into three sets of questions.

First, is the United States presently in a period of political dysfunction? What features or aspects of the political system evidence this dysfunction or are themselves dysfunctional?

Second, is there a better way to describe our current set of problems than political dysfunction?

Third, are our present problems caused by hard-wired features of the American Constitution, or are they caused by other features of the constitutional system? Is a constitutional amendment or a new constitutional convention the appropriate remedy for these problems, or would other kinds of remedies prove more effective or appropriate?

Is the Problem Dysfunction?

You begin by asserting that no one seriously doubts that the United States is currently in a period of political dysfunction. But I think the question is far more difficult. That is because the term "dysfunction" is quite ambiguous.

If dysfunction means that politicians are unable to perform the ordinary tasks of governance, it is by no means clear that the national government is dysfunctional. It all depends on whose perspective you are taking. The Debt Ceiling Crisis of 2011 caused enormous anxiety. Yet it led to the Budget Control Act of 2011, which, if you are a Republican, was an enormous policy success because it slowed the growth of federal spending. Again, if you are a Republican, you might well rejoice in the fact that the percentage of the workforce employed by federal, state, and local governments has significantly decreased during Barack Obama's presidency, although, as a Republican, you might be loath to give Obama credit for this.

If by dysfunction you mean that the president and Congress do not seem to agree on anything these days, the upcoming 2016 election would seem to provide an easy cure. Simply elect a Republican to the White House, end the legislative filibuster, and the problem is solved. Then the national government would be like many state governments with one-party rule. These governments are able to pass a great deal of legislation. Many of these reforms are ill-advised, but that does not mean that these state governments are dysfunctional. It means only that democratic governments sometimes produce very unwise policies.

Now if the thought of a Republican Congress working with President Trump, Rubio, or Jeb Bush disturbs you far more than the status quo, it is not clear to me that what you really are worried about is *dysfunction*. That is because you are presumably delighted that President Obama (and forty-six Democrats and independents in the Senate) stand ready to prevent Republicans from dismantling not only Obamacare, but large chunks of the New Deal and the modern welfare state. Rather, your real objection is to policies that you dislike. Your problem is that a substantial percentage of the American public disagrees with you about public policy and does not want the same things that you want. Your problem is not dysfunction—it is control (or blocking) by your political opponents.

Perhaps the problem boils down to the concern that the U.S. government is dysfunctional because (pending the results of the 2016 election) it is easier to push policies in a direction Republicans like, and it is harder to push them in a direction that many Democrats like. That may not in fact be true, but even if it were true, one would then have to couple this claim with the (contestable) assertion that the Democrats, for all their faults, are closer to the real or genuine interests of the public and of democracy generally, regardless of what the opinion polls say. But I am not sure that the best way to describe this state of affairs is political dysfunction.

Perhaps by dysfunction we mean polarized parties and irrespon-sible politicians. One might point to bitter ideological division be-tween the two major political parties, and to the remarkably irrespon-sible economic views held by one of them (I will not say which one!), which block a rational response to our current economic problems. Yet the United States weathered the greatest challenge of the past decade—the Great Recession—far better than most other Western democracies, including those with parliamentary systems that do not have the multiple veto points that the U.S. Constitution has. For all of the inanity of our political classes and the many veto points in our sys-tem, we must be doing *something* right.

Or we might identify dysfunction with lack of public trust in gov-ernment. One might point to the public's loss of trust in the federal government and the general sense (judging from recent public opin-ion polls) that the country is moving in the wrong direction. But as Stephen Griffin points out in his recent book on constitutional dys-function, *Broken Trust*, the public has been losing trust in government for many decades, going back to the 1960s. This decline began long before the period that one might assert is the present period of dys-function. Perhaps even more embarrassing, much of the decline be-gins during a period of great achievement for democracy and equality in the United States. It is precisely when government becomes more equal, fair, and open that Americans begin to lose trust in their gov-ernment. Pessimism about the country's general direction is not the same thing as lack of trust in government. Such pessimism about the country's general direction tends to fluctuate with the business cycle and with the state of the economy, and may also vary depending on party affiliation.

Finally, I should note that my own view, outlined in my 2014 essay "The Last Days of Disco," is that what we are calling "dysfunction" is actually a *transition* between constitutional or political regimes. Just as the New Deal/civil rights regime of the mid-twentieth century even-tually fell apart, the Republican regime that has dominated American politics since 1980 is nearing its end. [I explain the theory of political regimes and their rise and fall in my August 7, 2016, letter.]

Although the Republicans still control Congress and most state legislatures, the two parties are increasingly evenly matched, and demographic shifts, as well as a continuing civil war within the Re-publican Party, appear to be sapping the Republicans' long political dominance. Eventually a new regime will emerge, and when it does, people will stop complaining how dysfunctional our system is, just as they stopped complaining about dysfunction during Roosevelt's and Reagan's presidencies.

Calling our system "dysfunctional," then, may not clarify matters because it runs together several phenomena: (1) polarization; (2) venality; (3) idiocy; (4) ineffectiveness (given a particular political perspective or ideology); (5) lack of representativeness; and (6) transition between constitutional regimes. This brings me to the second question: Is there a better way to describe our current set of problems? I believe there is.

The Problem Is Democracy, Not Dysfunction

The term "dysfunction" suggests that some function of government is not working properly. But the term remains ambiguous until we specify what the relevant function is. Government might be dysfunctional because it does not function well as a *government*—for example, because it cannot make decisions, because it cannot appropriate and spend money, because it cannot raise or support troops, or because it cannot respond to crises like the Great Recession. I have suggested above that none of these are really the case. Or government might be dysfunctional because it fails at a different criterion: it does not function well as representative government.

The latter, I think, is the real issue. To be sure, our present degree of polarization and political conflict naturally causes people to confuse the question of representativeness with the question of efficacy, but the two questions are not the same. An efficacious government need not be representative, and it can feature a great deal of polarization and conflict. Indeed, an efficacious government can exacerbate polarization and conflict precisely because it is efficacious in a particular way or in a particular direction. During the Obama administration, for example, the government made significant reforms to the health care and financial systems; these reforms seem to have made polarization worse, not better. Conversely, a representative government that truly reflects the diverse opinions of Americans may not be particularly efficacious or efficient.

Moreover, if, as I believe, we are in a period of transition between political regimes, we should expect a considerable amount of angst about democracy and worries that government no longer works as well as it once did. These concerns tend to happen precisely during such periods of transition. Think of the period between 1928 and 1936, for example, or the period between 1978 and 1984. These worries, however, will likely resolve themselves over time as the Reagan regime breaks down and is replaced by a new regime—whether one dominated by Democrats or Republicans. If *that* is what people mean by dysfunction, it is only a temporary problem.

Nevertheless, there is a quite different concern that is wrapped up in our current anxieties. I believe that it is a real problem, one that needs a solution, and that it will not be solved simply by waiting things out. But this problem is not primarily a problem of efficacy or a problem of polarization, although it may exacerbate both phenomena.

The big problem that we face today is that our system of democratic representation is broken. The system of representation is not broken because it fails to produce winners and losers who claim to represent us. It produces plenty of winners and losers, and politicians endlessly insist that they are working the people's will and doing the people's business. Rather, the system of representation is broken because it is seriously undemocratic and unrepublican. It is undemocratic because it is not responsive to public opinion. It is unrepublican because it is not fairly representative, allows too much self-entrenching behavior, is deeply corrupt, and is not directed at the achievement of the public good.

To be sure, this *is* a kind of dysfunction. After all, one of the functions of a democratic government is to be democratic. The function of a republican government is to represent the public and serve the public good. Our current system of government is defective in both respects. But we should not confuse this kind of dysfunction with the claim that the government can't get certain things done. Thus, instead of talking generally about political dysfunction, we should focus on what is really at stake—democracy and republicanism. The question we should ask is what features of our current system are deeply and pathologically undemocratic or unrepublican.

You have been arguing about these issues for a long time, Sandy—long before the current controversies over government dysfunction. Indeed, even if our system of government was efficacious, I believe that you would still object that it is not sufficiently democratic. Our current political unhappiness merely gives you the opportunity to call for reforms that you would have advocated regardless of the public's

current degree of satisfaction (or dissatisfaction) with their government.

Your previous work has tended to equate the question of political
dysfunction with the question of how directly and rapidly our institutions respond to public opinion, and especially with how easy it is for
the public to change directions through legislation or through initiative or referendum. That is why you are skeptical of the presidential
veto, for example. But, as noted above, we should not run together
questions of democracy and representativeness with questions of efficacy. That is because relatively undemocratic and unrepresentative
systems can function very effectively. In many respects, the United
States has been undemocratic and unrepublican by today's standards
throughout most of its history. Although it sometimes functioned
quite badly—think only of the period leading up to the Civil War—it
also often functioned quite well. (Indeed, if you think that the Jacksonian era was a period of increasing democracy, that was also the
period that brought us closer to civil war.)

I agree with you that there are features of our political system that
are deeply and unfairly undemocratic. The most important is our system of campaign finance and, relatedly, our system of lobbying and
access to representatives. A second problem is the urgent need to reform our representational and voting systems. Even without reforming the malapportioned Senate, there is much we could do to reorga-
nize democratic politics, make registration and voting easier, and
increase participation.

These undemocratic and unrepublican features of our system do
not necessarily make it dysfunctional from the standpoint of efficacy.
There have been long periods of time in the United States in which
wealth and capital dominated political agendas and in which either
a large percentage of ordinary people were disenfranchised or their
votes and voices were unfairly neglected and ignored. These periods
of time include periods that most people would not consider dysfunctional, even though there was also a significant amount of party polarization.

I also do not think that reforming campaign finance and voting will necessarily make government more efficient or effective. It
may or may not lead to wiser decisions. These reforms may not make
polarization go away or increase public trust. If Griffin is right, then

making government more accountable and transparent may actually increase public distrust. I am not at all sure that these reforms will prevent showdowns like the confrontations we have seen in the past eight years. What they will tend to produce is not less dysfunction, but more democracy—or at least a more fairly representative government.

Perhaps equally important, even if we focus on the question of democracy as opposed to efficacy, you and I might disagree about different features of our system and their relative importance. For example, I do not find the presidential veto a particularly serious problem, while you do. I do not think that moving up the date of Inauguration Day is all that important, while you have repeatedly pointed to it as a defect of our Constitution. Finally, although I agree that the Senate is drastically malapportioned, I do not think that abolishing it is a very high priority, while it is a major concern of yours. I might choose a different mix of reforms: some might be more "republican"—seeking to improve representation in different areas, preventing self-entrenchment, and rooting out political corruption. Others might be more "democratic"—facilitating mass participation and the practical ability to vote.

Is the Hard-Wired Constitution the Problem?

These differences in priorities bring me to the third set of questions. Are the anti-democratic (or anti-republican) features of our government primarily caused by hard-wired features of the U.S. Constitution or by other causes? And what is the appropriate remedy for these problems?

Here it is important to make a distinction between the constitutional order and the hard-wired Constitution. The constitutional order is the entire set of rules, doctrines, and practices that structure political decision making in the United States. The hard-wired Constitution consists of those rules embedded in the document that cannot be changed except by constitutional amendment.

Your work has tended to equate constitutional reform with altering the hard-wired Constitution. This requires either an Article V amendment—which, in turn, requires agreement by two-thirds of both houses of Congress and ratification by both houses in three-quarters of the state legislatures—or a new constitutional convention, whose

proposals would also have to be ratified by the states. That may be because you think that the most important problems with the Constitution come from its hard-wired features.

By contrast, I do not believe that the most serious problems with
our system come from its hard-wired features. Most of the constitutional order is not hard-wired. Therefore, I also do not believe that the
most important reforms to our constitutional order require Article V
amendment or a new constitutional convention. I have no objection to
either—I am not, like some of our colleagues, an amendment-phobe
or a convention-phobe. It is just that I do not believe that these are
the appropriate cure. We can reform many features of our constitutional system through statutory changes. For example, we can move
from single-member districts in the House to other forms by ordinary
statute. States can change their voting, registration, and redistricting
systems without a federal constitutional amendment. Even some features of the system that seem hard-wired, like the Electoral College,
can be worked around through ordinary politics. For example, states
can bargain around the Electoral College through an interstate compact ratified by Congress. To be sure, pushing for new amendments or
a new convention may raise public support for statutory or administrative solutions that do not require supermajority votes in the Congress
and the states. So pushing for amendments may sometimes be politically advantageous to achieving strategies that do not require amendments.

Another example is the current dysfunction in the House of Representatives, in which the Speaker is repeatedly forced to engage in
political brinksmanship before finally allowing essential legislation to
pass with Democratic votes. The problem stems from internal rules
of the Republican caucus. The Hastert Rule, for example, is a political convention under which the Speaker of the House refuses to allow
a vote on legislation supported by a majority of the House unless a
majority of his or her party's caucus also supports it. In addition, current House rules effectively prevent any Republican Speaker from
being elected without the consent of the House's Freedom Caucus;
this holds the Speaker hostage to the House's most ideologically extreme elements.

These difficulties are not due to the hard-wired Constitution. Although Article I, Section 2, Clause 5 of the Constitution prescribes
that "the House of Representatives shall choose their Speaker and

other Officers," it does not specify how this is to be accomplished. There are any number of non-constitutional reforms that would prevent the current system of dysfunction we are witnessing in the House.

Some reforms, especially in the area of campaign finance, may require changes in constitutional doctrine. Constitutional amendment is probably the least effective way to achieve them. Changing doctrine normally requires that judges change their minds or, more likely, that new presidents appoint new judges. If one amends the Constitution but leaves the same judges in place, there is the risk that the judges will neuter the changes. That is why Franklin Roosevelt decided to focus on new judicial appointments instead of Article V amendments.

I agree with you that law professors tend to focus obsessively on the work of judges and pay less attention to questions of constitutional design. I agree that they should shift more of their attention to questions of constitutional design. It does not follow, however, that they should shift their attention to Article V amendment, much less to a new constitutional convention. Rather, they should focus on features of the constitutional order that can be modified both at the state and federal levels by a combination of legislative, administrative, and doctrinal reforms.

Jack

OCTOBER 12, 2015

Dear Jack,

As always, you raise a number of excellent questions. We may disagree
less than you think, but our disagreements are certainly important. Indeed, in the interim between my first letter and this one, the House of
Representatives has been thrown into chaos by the joint phenomena
of the apparent resignation by Speaker John Boehner and the seeming
inability of the Republican caucus to agree on a successor who in fact
is willing to take that thankless job. [Since these comments were written, the Republicans did settle on Paul Ryan to be Speaker, where he
remains in 2018, though he has announced his intention to retire from
the House at the conclusion of his present term.]

Let me address your three points in turn:

"Functionality" and "Dysfunctionality"

First, as to the meaning of "dysfunctionality," you are absolutely
right. Perhaps, like most terms that we throw about in our political
discourse—think also of such favorites as "democratic" or "republican" forms of government—"functionality" and "dysfunctionality" are
what political theorists call "essentially contested concepts." The importance of such concepts lies not only in the fact that smart people
of good faith in many cases have disagreed for literally centuries about
their meanings, but also that there are positive or negative valences
attached to the terms themselves. Although in the eighteenth century,
relatively few theorists were willing to be identified as proponents of

"democracy," in the twenty-first century, its desirability is taken as a given, especially in what we still call "the West." It has become common to judge existing countries by the degree to which they are sufficiently "democratic" and, perhaps, even to intervene and overthrow existing leaders in the name of furthering "democracy." So something rides, practically speaking, on whether a particular system is identified as democratic or undemocratic; it is not surprising, then, that partisans of one or another particular country (including the United States, of course) will fix on self-serving definitions of democracy, even as their adversaries proclaim what may be quite different (and perhaps equally self-serving) alternatives.

But I also want to say some specific things about "functionality" and "dysfunctionality." Any supporter of an existing political order wants to be able to describe it as functional, even as opponents will claim just the opposite. The key issue is what set of expectations or criteria we use to measure functionality. Were we talking about human life, for example, we could define it quite minimally in terms of being able to sustain oneself as a biological entity. If, on the other hand, one includes notions of "flourishing" in addition to what might be termed "mere survival," one would come up with a quite different analysis. Apartheid South Africa was altogether functional in maintaining the hegemony of what was termed "Herrenvolk democracy," the domination of a majority black population by whites, primarily Afrikaners, though certainly joined by many of British descent. If one, on the other hand, sympathized with the African National Congress and others fighting for the rights of the beleaguered majority, one would not praise the functionality of the tyranny created especially after 1948.

Your eminent Yale colleague David Mayhew is famous for arguing that Congress is far more functional than many of us believe, and he proffers as evidence the fact that even in times of divided government it is able to pass legislation, some of it quite important. In his 2013 book, *Partisan Balance: Why Political Parties Don't Kill the U.S. Constitutional System*, he lists an impressive number of bills that were passed during the 1980s and 1990s, when neither Democrats nor Republicans were able to gain control of both branches of Congress plus the White House. No one should ever dispute the accuracy of Mayhew's numbers; he is stunningly erudite about American politics. That being said, though, I have in my own book *Framed* criticized Mayhew inasmuch as he seems to regard the list as a "knock-down argument." I believe, on the contrary, that he is insufficiently attentive to the limitations of the legislation he cites with regard to confronting in satisfactory measure the depth of the challenges facing us as a country. Not all legislation, obviously, is *good* legislation even if, as a political scientist, one might agree that it was the best that might have been hoped for given the institutional contexts within which the American political system operates.

And even Mayhew, incidentally, has agreed that the contemporary Congress is quite different in major respects from the halcyon days of the 1980s and 1990s. By any account, far less legislation is being passed. The Voice of America news itself reported in December 2013 that "the 113th Congress has been the least productive in history, with the House and Senate passing only 57 bills that were signed into law by President Barack Obama," and it correctly predicted that things would get no better in the election year of 2014. Republicans, of course, took over the Senate in 2015. To be sure, Congress toward the end of 2015 was able to pass a bill designed to keep the government functioning without another shutdown, but this is surely to adopt an absolute minimal standard for what counts as congressional functionality. Indeed, the Republican Senate during 2016 is perhaps most noteworthy for quite literally refusing to hold a single day of hearings on the nomination by President Obama of Judge Merrick Garland to succeed Antonin Scalia, who had died in February 2016.

In any event, to put on a Band-Aid may count, from one perspective, as responding to an injury, but if major surgery is actually required, it would be quixotic to offer the Band-Aid as evidence of a sufficient response, even if it was the best medical treatment actually available. Admittedly, we may be far more often confident about medical diagnoses and treatment plans than about politics. We often disagree about our most basic descriptions of the political world (is there really a phenomenon called "global warming" and, even if there is, is there a causal connection to presumptively changeable behavior by human beings?); but agreement on the diagnosis may lead to almost endless political warfare about what count as adequate responses. We are increasingly likely to disagree on the treatment plans, often combining at that stage particularly both factual assertions—"it will never work or, indeed, be counterproductive"—with value statements as well—"it might work, but only at the price of depriving us of our liberty or our prosperity."

In any event, it should be absolutely clear that one simply cannot present a neutral notion of functionality or dysfunctionality without at the very same instant taking a political position. The Affordable Care Act is a fine example of governmental functioning at its best if and only if one agrees with enough of its factual and value premises. Ditto your own example of the "solution" to the Debt Ceiling Crisis of 2011, which gave us, among other things, the lunatic "policy" (scare quotes intended) of the sequester, which takes an almost literally mindless cleaver to almost all government programs.

It is true, though, that I am mixing up two decidedly different notions of functionality and dysfunctionality, and you are right to call me out on it. That is, with regard to the American polity since the take-over of the House by Republicans in 2011, a basic reality is the near impossibility of passing *any* significant legislation. We have embraced a culture of low expectations by giving Congress credit for managing, at the last minute, to prevent defaulting on the national debt, even though the machinations required to avoid default triggered a lowering by Standard & Poor's of the credit-worthiness of the United States from the "gold standard" AAA to AA+. And in doing so, incidentally, Standard & Poor's referred not to the weakness of the U.S. economy, still the world's strongest, but, rather, to doubts that had developed about the adequacy of our political system. They were correct.

So take your question: Would the election of, say, Ted Cruz bring functionality back to American politics by leading to the passage of all sorts of wondrous legislation by an invigorated Republican majority in the House and Senate, which would eagerly be signed by President Cruz? The answer is clearly yes, if all we mean by functionality is the ability of Congress to pass legislation. Perhaps this is the equivalent of praising the German army for functioning so well in the blitzkrieg of 1939, when it quickly conquered Poland before moving on to France. But, obviously, the second, and perhaps more controversial, aspect of defining functionality and dysfunctionality now comes into play, for we must necessarily ask what actually is being achieved, whether by legislation or by armies. Or, perhaps, we must recognize that functionality along one dimension, whether legislative or military, must be placed within the context of the wider system and also recognize the extent to which the functionality in a limited domain leads overall to what we regard as a functional or dysfunctional political order.

Still, even there, values will necessarily come into play. Surely most of us believe that Germany became a dysfunctional political order well before late 1944 and 1945 when its leaders recognized that they had so totally lost control of events that unilateral surrender (and suicide) were the only viable options. For some of us, a "unitary government" fashioned by a Cruz-dominated Republican coalition would be enough to despair about the future of the United States (and the world) and to entertain thoughts not only of emigration but, far more seriously, of secession. Why would we expect Pacifica—composed of California, Oregon, and Washington, perhaps joined by Hawaii—to remain within such a Union? A serious secessionist movement, as distinguished from the "let's pretend" versions that are rife within the United States, would, presumably, be evidence of dysfunctionality. But is that what it would take to overcome your argument that the Cruz regime, however obnoxious, would demonstrate a capacity to govern that would overcome the dysfunction-oriented analyses like my own?

"Representation" and "Democracy"

I begin with the titles of two books of mine: *Our Undemocratic Constitution: Where the Constitution Goes Wrong (and How We the People Can Correct It)* and then *Framed: America's 51 Constitutions and the Crisis of Governance.* The first one, obviously, addresses whether the Constitution of 1787, left remarkably unamended in relevant structural aspects, could possibly be described as democratic using fairly routine twenty-first-century standards of democracy. My answer is a resolute no, where the basis of comparison is not only other constitutions from around the world but, far more relevantly, the constitutions of the fifty states. Each of the fifty states has its own constitution; all of them are more democratic than their national counterpart, not least because of the reapportionment decisions by the Supreme Court in the 1960s that eliminated what was called "little federalism," by which at least one house of a bicameral legislature could in effect mimic the U.S. Senate in its glaring departure from population equality. But the response to that book led me to the conclusion that most people in fact adopted the equivalent of a "so what?" attitude toward such demonstrable departures from contemporary democratic theory.

Many correctly pointed out that the framers were scarcely twenty-first-century democrats, and that was really fine. As the John Birch

Society put it in the 1960s, "We're a republic, not a democracy, and
let's keep it that way." Even more to the point, for many, is that our system was working at least "well enough" to warrant praise rather than
snarky condemnation based on academic conceptions of democracy.
The word "democracy" is capable of describing a house with many dif-
ferently hued rooms, and what obtains in the United States is certainly
one of them, even if my own taste is considerably different.

Thus the change in the later book, with its emphasis on "the crisis of
governance." That there *is* such a crisis now seems to be widely agreed;
this is just what it means to express deep worry about the dysfunctionality of the American political system. But you describe at least
some elements of this crisis as likely to be quite transient, as discussed
above. Still, it might well be the case that a more "democratic" system—defined for our purposes as one in which the national government faithfully reflects the policy views of electoral majorities inasmuch as the minority no longer enjoys access to veto points that can
block the instantiation of these views—would itself generate such unhappiness as to lead to a far deeper crisis of governance. This could be
manifested by any genuine movement toward secession or the greater
frequency of mass movements coupled literally with rioting in the
streets. Regime change is no small matter, especially if the proposed
changes are deep and pervasive rather than relatively marginal. The
Reagan Revolution looks quite tame compared with the visions of the
Freedom Caucus within the House of Representatives and others who
might demand a great deal of effective say should a Republican win
the White House in 2016.

As the great Robert Dahl argued many years ago, democracy of
the American type, i.e., composed of great numbers of diverse citizens (and, for that matter, non-citizens), is always subject to the problems posed by groups who are *intensely* antagonistic to one another
and therefore indisposed to the compromises that are thought to be
necessary to pluralistic polities. To overcome these baleful possibilities, Dahl took refuge in the reality of "cross-cutting" cleavages, where
individuals were members of many different groups and organizations
that would put them in contact with individuals like them in some
respects—their liking for public support of culture, whether high or
low—and very different in others, such as their relative support for re-
productive choice as against the right to life.

It has certainly been argued that an important development over the past several decades, even as the total American population has in many ways become ever more diverse, is the diminution of such cross-cutting cleavages. People seem to be sorting themselves out more by reference to their major modes of identification, even without conscious political gerrymandering, which reduces the possibility that centrist voters, pulled in different directions by their cross-cutting associations, will dominate the electoral process. Perhaps the most vivid evidence of this was provided by electoral maps following the 2012 presidential election. Relatively few counties or, for that matter, congressional districts were divided 51–47 percent between Barack Obama and Mitt Romney, even though that was the national vote percentage. States themselves deviated quite dramatically, of course. Texas, for example, where I live, gave 57.2 percent of its votes to Romney. But even within Texas, very few counties tracked the statewide percentages. Instead, Travis County, the home of the University of Texas, where I teach, gave 60.2 percent of its votes to Obama even as most other counties were giving 70 and even 80 percent of their votes to Governor Romney. In the battleground state of Ohio, won by Obama with 51.1 percent of the popular vote, Obama obtained 68 percent of the vote in Cuyahoga County (Cleveland) and 60 percent of the vote in Franklin County (Columbus), though Romney carried a number of far smaller, rural counties by even more impressive margins.

These differences within states also help to explain the particular reality of the modern House of Representatives and the importance, for example, of the call by Fair Vote for repealing the congressional statute, dating back to 1842, that mandates single-member districts. Instead, we could require relatively large states (those with, say, more than seven representatives) to elect them in multi-member districts using proportional representation. Among other things, this brings home the degree to which our very definition of majority rule (assuming we think that such rule is a good thing) is created in part by formal institutions and the incentives they generate with regard, for example, to the creation and maintenance of our particular two-party system.

But what this also suggests, among other things, is the tension within American political and constitutional thought between adhering to the wishes of majorities—even if those wishes are, as Justice Oliver Wendell Holmes put it in his *Lochner* dissent, "tyrannical"— and instead being disciplined by the demands of overarching constitutional norms, or what Publius repeatedly invoked in *The Federal-*

ist as "the public good" (or Michael Sandel, a leading contemporary proponent of "civic republican" politics, describes as "the common good"). Yet, as many people, including Dahl, have pointed out, Publius is Janus-faced, for he also emphasized the ubiquitous elements of self-seeking and raw ambition as constituting our politics, and he ultimately relied more on "ambition counteracting ambition" than on the homilies contained in "parchment barriers," including the Bill of Rights, to discipline political leaders.

Publius was desperately trying to prevent the creation of a party system, a system that, by definition, means that members of a given party must on occasion subordinate their own notions of the public interest to the interests of their party. He failed completely and unequivocally, with mixed consequences. There are many good reasons to have political parties; furthermore, no serious person believes in the possibility of truly nonpartisan politics. Perhaps this is not true for the partisans of particular monarchs or dictators who argue that they have remarkable capacities for discerning the needs of their people. Benevolent despotism is still available as a theory, even if there are few advocates. But we must recognize that there is no such thing as a free lunch, and partisan politics certainly brings defects to government, sometimes very serious ones. These defects must be tamed by some notion of subordination to a general good, even at the cost of party advantage in the next election.

The "Hard-Wired Constitution" (or the Constitution of Settlement)

You continue to be far more optimistic than I am that the United States can escape from its winter, spring, summer, and fall of its discontent by ingenious (or ingenuous) "workarounds" of the more dismal features of the system bequeathed us in Philadelphia and left quite impervious to change because of the truly dreadful Article V that structures constitutional amendment itself. You refer to Stephen Griffin's excellent new book, and one of Griffin's suggestions is that we would be far better off as a political (and constitutional) order if the national government gave the same opportunity to its citizens that is available in many American states (and foreign countries) to engage in at least some measure of direct democracy through the initiative and referendum.

I will not rehearse all of my arguments as to why constitutional re-form might be both necessary and proper. As the dedicatee of *Framed*, you are well aware of all of my arguments, and readers can obviously track them down with ease. What I do wish to assert, in ending my second missive in this exchange, is that the very worst consequence of Article V is that it has infantilized our politics by making it impossible, as a practical matter, to have serious discussions about constitutional reform. Frankly, only zealots would devote their scarce time, money, and energy to proposals necessitating constitutional change. The "amendment game" is simply stacked too much in favor of the status quo. Elizabeth Warren speaks of the game being "rigged" with regard to banks and certain business corporations; this is even truer with re-gard to the Constitution itself. If one is faced with rigged games, the most rational response, assuming that revolutionary overthrow is im-possible, is simply to do something else and to tell oneself that the game is not really all that important anyhow.

I do *not* think that waiting until January to inaugurate a new presi-dent is the most serious weakness in the Constitution; only a true zealot could possibly think that. But I do think that you underesti-mate the potential costs of the hiatus that has regularly been inflicted on the country where an insurgent candidate either defeats the in-cumbent (Roosevelt in 1932, Reagan in 1980) or decisively defeats the coalition presided over by the incumbent, even if he is not formally on the ballot (Lincoln in 1860, Clinton in 1992, Obama in 2008). [One might add Trump's defeat of Clinton in 2016 to this list.] It is no small matter for the United States to have an ineffective president in the time between the discredited incumbent and the legitimate insurgent. But even something so banal as moving up Inauguration Day is un-discussed and thought impossible. The reason may simply be that it would necessarily require confronting the perverse Electoral College, opposed by every Gallup poll taken since 1944, but still structuring our presidential elections and creating the dreadful phenomenon of battleground states that distort our entire polity.

It is true, as you point out, that the Electoral College could in effect be neutralized through adoption of the Fair Vote proposal, by which the ten largest states would agree to allocate their votes to the winner of the popular vote. It is worth noting though that it would not at all af-fect the potential costs of the delayed inauguration, even if one stilled any doubts about the wisdom of the Fair Vote proposal itself (which does not, importantly, require that the "winner" in fact demonstrate majority support as against simply coming in first past the post in the national totals).[1]

The real point is that I almost desperately want a national conversation about the weaknesses, and strengths, of our basic constitutional system and the degree to which the rigidities of the written Constitution—coupled with what John Ferejohn and William Eskridge have termed "constitutionalized statutes," including the requirement of single-member districts—require explicit textual amendment and not simply clever workarounds. We would be having such conversations—and possibly even conventions—if, as is the case in fourteen states in the Union, the Constitution's text mandated that the electorate be given the opportunity, at stated intervals (usually ten or twenty years), to vote on whether or not to have a new constitutional convention. Perhaps it is a bit like an assisted suicide statute; one may very well never use the life-ending drug supplied by a physician, but it is a great comfort to know the possibility is there and that, therefore, one is more genuinely in control of one's life, including the inevitable leave-taking. Whatever the promise of the Constitution's Preamble about the importance of "We the People," the reality is something else, and I, for one, would feel much better if the citizenry were not forced to continue living under a greatly defective Constitution because our doctors, in 1787, deprived us of an effective way of reasserting our own collective autonomy.

I will stop for now, secure in the belief that you will offer thoughtful responses to all of these points.

Sandy

---

1. One should recognize the significance of the facts, for example, that Lincoln came to office with only 39.8 percent of the popular vote and that both Richard Nixon in 1968 and Bill Clinton in 1992 prevailed by gaining 43 percent of the popular vote. This is considerably different from the functional "tie vote" between Bush and Gore in 2000.

NOVEMBER 1, 2015

Dear Sandy,

You freely acknowledge that your view that our constitutional system is dysfunctional is shaped by your political preferences. We might compare your approach to constitutional dysfunction to that of the Progressives in the early twentieth century. Their demand for constitutional reform was propelled by a substantive agenda, combined with the sense that the old Constitution blocked desirable change. The Progressive political scientist Henry Jones Ford famously spoke of the Progressive vision of the presidency as "the work of the people, breaking through the constitutional form." In much the same way, you want to break through our present-day constitutional forms to reenergize government and achieve reforms that, in your opinion, the country desperately needs.

Of course, as soon as you link your calls for constitutional reform to a particular (progressive) substantive agenda, you will likely lose support from people who do not agree with your politics. And that may make it very hard to obtain supermajority support in Congress and in the states.

As you have pointed out, Tea Party conservatives are also quite interested in constitutional reform. They simply seek different reforms than you do, and with different ends than yours. Nevertheless, what you and the Tea Party share is the belief that constitutional reform is not inconsistent with the best parts of the American political tradition. Quite the contrary, as Publius argues in the opening essay of *The Federalist*, making our system of government a matter of "reflection and choice" is and should be the most characteristically American enterprise. But where many Tea Party acolytes regard much of twentieth-century constitutional development as a mistake and seek a kind of constitutional restoration, you hope to move the Constitution in an even more Progressive (in both senses of the word) direction.

This helps explain your view that a unified federal government under the leadership of the current Republican Party might be dysfunctional under your definition of that term. Offering a comparison to the German blitzkrieg at the beginning of World War II, you argue that political efficiency in the service of a disastrous political agenda is not an efficiency worth having. Yet this concern is the classic justification for the very features of our constitutional system that you would like to reform. The American Constitution has multiple veto points and checks and balances precisely to prevent the kind of calamity that you fear would occur if your political adversaries were able to work their will without restraint. So it is a bit odd for you to offer these concerns in your explanation of why our constitutional system is dysfunctional. Put another way, I do not think one can simultaneously argue that the Constitution is dysfunctional if it prevents progressives from pursuing agendas that they believe are in the public interest, but that it is also dysfunctional if it fails to prevent conservatives from pursuing their agendas.

But perhaps there is a better way to make your point. You suggest that if a firebrand like Ted Cruz were elected in 2016, and if the Republicans retained majorities in both houses of Congress, liberal states in the Pacific West might consider secession. A central function of a constitution is, as I like to say, to "make politics possible." A well-functioning constitution establishes a political order that gives people incentives to resolve their disputes through politics and protest rather than through violence and civil war. So, you might argue, if significant parts of the country have lost faith that they will eventually be able to get a fair shake through ordinary politics, there is something deeply wrong with the Constitution. And if a constitution cannot keep a political union together, it is to that extent a failure. Thus, the argument might go, the problem is not that you find the policies of a unified Republican government objectionable. Rather, the problem is that such a government will lead to dissolution of the Union, which is evidence of constitutional failure. In the same way, you might point out, even if Abraham Lincoln's election in 1860 was a very good thing for the

United States, the fact that various states seceded in 1861 is proof that the 1787 Constitution had failed at its most central function.

Fair enough. But I think that there is very little evidence that any part of the country would attempt to secede—much less actually achieve independence—if the Republican Party gained the presidency and both houses of Congress, as it did only a decade ago during George W. Bush's administration. One of the most interesting features of our present polarized politics is how remarkably little widespread political unrest there has been to date. (I include protests against police misconduct by groups like Black Lives Matter.) Moreover, even if the Pacific states wanted to leave, it is simply not feasible for a superpower like the United States to permit a potentially hostile country to form on its western border, especially if that country would retain a powerful military and any degree of nuclear power. I think it is safe to say that, at least at this point in its history, the United States will not consent to the exit of any state from the Union. Of course, this may change in the future, but it would be under very different circumstances—when the United States was so debilitated that it was no longer a major world power and could no longer enforce its will within its own borders. For example, secession might occur if the United States had been successfully invaded by another power, or if an economic crisis left the central government unable to provide basic services to or defend parts of the country. That is not the situation today. For this reason, I do not think you have made the case that a unified government led by Republicans is dysfunctional because it may lead to secession. It may lead to very unwise policies, but those are not the same thing as dysfunction.

One should not, however, let disputes about the concept of dysfunction get in the way of your larger point. You argue that "the very worst consequence of Article V is that it has infantilized our politics by making it impossible, as a practical matter, to have serious discussions about constitutional reform." I agree with you that it is important for Americans to have serious discussions about constitutional reform, especially in today's circumstances. I disagree with you that Article V stands in the way of serious discussion.

Constitutional reform involves the constituent power of the people—the power of "We the People"—to establish a constitution and alter or amend it. But we should not assume that the constituent power of the people is reserved only to "great and extraordinary occasions," as *Federalist* No. 49 puts it. Rather, much contemporary constitutional theory, including theories that you have championed, argues that the constituent power of the people can be and often is exercised outside of Article V. Both Bruce Ackerman's work on constitutional moments and my work on constitutional construction are premised on the idea that "We the People" engage in constitutional change outside of Article V. Ackerman argues that Americans have worked around the state-centered rules of Article V amendment and developed national models for constitutional amendment. I have argued that through state-building constructions by the political branches and judicial constructions by the courts, Americans have repeatedly changed the Constitution-in-practice.

I believe that you should integrate your earlier work on constitutional amendment with your present work on constitutional design. The two fit together very well.

How is it possible to have constitutional reform without Article V amendment? As I pointed out in my initial response, it is crucial to distinguish between the hard-wired Constitution and the constitutional order. Although the hard-wired Constitution requires Article V amendment, the constitutional order can be altered through many different methods. These include ordinary legislation, changes in the internal rules of the Senate and House, constitutional workarounds, and state compacts—such as the reform of the Electoral College I mentioned previously. They also include new judicial appointments and new judicial doctrines that might limit or overrule previous decisions and uphold new campaign finance and voting reforms. If America does change its campaign finance and electoral systems, I expect that most of the reforms, if not all of them, will occur outside of Article V amendment.

I do not pretend that every reform to our constitutional system can be achieved outside of Article V. We cannot, for example, move Inauguration Day to the second week of November (although, of course, we could create a set of political conventions that ameliorated the problem if the outgoing and incoming administrations cooperated). But this does not strike me as a major source of our current difficulties. Rather, as discussed in my first essay, our most pressing problems concern our system of representation. We can address most of these through the methods of constitutional construction I have listed above. And many other problems that we currently associate with political dysfunction will recede as we transition to a new constitutional regime.

My central disagreement with your approach is that you too easily run together constitutional reform with Article V amendment or with a new constitutional convention. Doing so exacerbates the very problem of "infantilization" that you complain about. It leads people to believe that they can only change their political institutions through Article V or through a new convention, which, in turn, leads to despair and resignation. Yet constitutional reform is not the same thing as Article V amendment. Amendment is only one path. If you actually want constitutional reform to move outside of the seminar room and into political discussion, you should accept and emphasize this way of framing the issue.

Although the nation seems mired in gridlock, political conditions are not permanent. They change. This fact should give us hope that it is worth making the effort. Even if progress is slow at first, the course of American history demonstrates, over and over again, that political persistence can pay off. And when change comes, it is often rapid, although the previous struggles and preparations that make change possible often take many years. The reforms of the Progressive Era were many decades in the making; so too were the changes of the New Deal and the civil rights revolution. Some of the political reforms our country needs will come through Article V amendment; but many, perhaps most, will not. That is the central lesson that people should draw from our history.

There is no reason why Americans should despair that their generation cannot also be one of great achievement. You have often pointed out, correctly, that blind reverence for the Constitution is a great failing. But faith in the possibility of progress is not blind reverence; and faith in the adaptability of our constitutional system is our greatest asset.

Jack

PART TWO

DYSFUNCTION AND

THE RISE OF

DONALD TRUMP

AUGUST 1, 2016

Dear Jack,

The first thing the reader will notice, of course, is that our first two letters were written within what Aristotle might have called a relative unity of time, whereas this new exchange begins more than a full eight months later than your November 1st response to my prior letter. Even more important than the lag per se is the fact that we are now writing after the conclusions of the Republican and Democratic national conventions and their respective nominations of Donald Trump and Hillary Clinton for the presidency.

To put it mildly, much has happened since what now appear the almost-halcyon days of November, when we were in Indianapolis. As John Lennon sang, "Life is what happens to you while you're busy making other plans"; one can say with confidence that many of those who made plans as to what the 2016 election would be like, particularly at the presidential level, have found them nearly irrelevant. In Indianapolis, we were talking about whether Paul Ryan could in fact tame the recalcitrant Freedom Caucus within the House. Should Donald Trump become president, that might literally be the least of Ryan's worries!

Rather than engage in prognostications that will be of little interest several months from now, let me offer some wider-ranging comments on the constitutional significance of the election battle, especially in terms of our overarching debate about the contribution of the Constitution to our political discontents.

I note that I am deeply disappointed (and more than a bit angry) at

Bernie Sanders, *not* for running against Hillary Clinton, whom in fact I supported, but, rather, for posturing as a "political revolutionary." But not once, even for a millisecond, did he suggest that any serious revolution would require engaging first in what Publius called serious "reflection" about the adequacy of the Constitution in the twenty-first century and then in a collective "choice" to change things, as was done so notably in 1787. Sanders never bothered to inform his impressionable followers that his promises, whatever their merit, had almost zero chance of actual adoption because of the structures adopted in 1787. What he was doing, in his own way, was imitating Donald Trump by pretending in effect that presidents could wave magic wands and make things happen. On occasion, as in certain aspects of foreign and military policy, that might be true; with regard to domestic affairs, it is remarkably untrue, as Hillary Clinton learned to her dismay when living in the White House with her husband and attempting to reform the American medical services industry. She is often criticized for the relative "prose" of her campaign, in contrast to the "poetry" that often characterizes her opponents, whether Obama in 2008 or Sanders or even Trump in 2016. Mario Cuomo famously declared that one campaigns in poetry, but must govern in prose. Perhaps she learned that all "poetry" does is raise expectations that cannot possibly be met, which leads, almost inexorably, to further disillusionment and alienation.

And here is where I continue to ride my hobbyhorse of wanting us to pay attention to the Constitution itself and at least to think of serious constitutional reform. Our overemphasis on the candidates and the promises they make has led us to the over-personalization of politics, the belief that everything will be all right if only we get the right leader or, concomitantly, that what is going wrong can be blamed on the deficiencies of the leaders we have. We end up adopting a version of the "great man" (or "woman") theory of history, reinforced by the general emphasis, especially of history written for a general audience, on presidents as heroes or villains.

I do not want to deny the importance of individuals. I do think it was important that we had presidents with the political skills and moral imagination of Abraham Lincoln and Franklin Roosevelt. But I think that we ignore the importance of underlying structures—or, for that matter, of the political cultures and social movements that placed Lincoln and Roosevelt in office and gave them support—at our peril. I personally view Donald Trump as a narcissistic sociopath who simply must be beaten. It would be an utter calamity for the United States and for the entire world if he became our president. [He did, of course, win, and it *has* been calamitous.]

But enough of speculation about the future. What I want to conclude with are some musings answering the following question: Should we really be so completely shocked at the rise of someone like Donald Trump as a potential president (rather than, say, as a candidate for the House or Senate)? I think that Max Weber, the great German political sociologist, had much to teach us in a 1918 essay that he wrote in the aftermath of World War I and the transformation of Germany from an authoritarian monarchy to a presumably more democratic political system. Weber suggested that all systems of "direct election by the people of the bearer of supreme power" have within them an impulse (perhaps today, we should use the metaphor of a "gene") toward Caesarism. It is, of course, a notable truth about the 1787 Constitution that it explicitly rejected proposals for direct election in favor of what I strongly believe to be the inanity of the Electoral College. But the original theory, if not the played-out reality, of the Electoral College was not so inane. One might imagine the electors as the original superdelegates, chosen by the legislature or by the electorate to exercise independent judgment as to who would best serve the interests of the Union. That vision of the Electoral College, whatever one thinks of it, has long since collapsed. Contemporary electors serve no useful purpose as genuine filters between popular sentiment and presidential selection. They are expected simply to mirror the preferences of the dominant parties in their states, who need not even amass a majority of the vote should a third-party candidate take sufficient votes away from the two major-party candidates. Maine and Nebraska at least do not follow the winner-take-all principle, but still give electors no real judgment. Indeed, we refer to electors who do think for themselves as rogues, though, fortunately, none has been truly consequential in choosing a president.[1]

1. Indeed, following the election, I endorsed the possibility of such roguery! See Sanford Levinson, Jeremi Suri, and Jeffrey Tulis, "The Hail Mary Pass That Could Deny Donald Trump the Presidency: It's Up to You, Electors," *New York Daily News*, November 21, 2016, http://www.nydailynews.com/opinion/tulis-levinson-suri-hail-mary-defeat-donald-trump-article-1.2882315 [https://perma.cc/GE7N-TDUG] (calling on patriotic electors to unite in providing the House of Representatives with an alterna-

The great alternative to direct election, of course, is parliamentary designation, in which the "bearer of supreme power" is always vulnerable to the parliamentary majority. Political parties can claim "mandates," but in a properly functioning parliamentary system, prime ministers cannot claim personal mandates that override the wishes of their parties or coalitions that placed them in power. But, of course, the United States, unlike most developed countries in the world today, has resolutely rejected parliamentarianism in favor of a byzantine system of separation of powers, which explains the phenomenon of the 2016 election season. At the very least, this is a subject worth discussing in the constitutional convention that I continue to hope we have. Indeed, it would be a worthy topic should the voters of New York exercise their constitutionally granted powers (under the New York State Constitution) to vote in 2017 to call a new convention to discuss amending that constitution.[2] States have totally failed to serve as "little laboratories of experimentation" with regard to presenting alternatives to separation of powers, which is a real shame.

In any event, the phenomenon of Donald Trump may be an illustration, dreadful but accurate, of the Weberian analysis. The sociopathic, narcissistic Trump is running a classically "Caesarist" campaign, relying on large rallies and whipping up crowds by the use of bombastic claims that ultimately rely on the premise that he alone can "make America great again." It was George W. Bush who emphasized that he alone was "the decider." Trump is building on that image of the presidency.

In all fairness, though, one should not assume that Weber's analysis kicks in only this year, without any such inklings prior to this dreadful political year (or to the Bush-Cheney regime). My colleague Jeff Tulis has written a seminal book, *The Rhetorical Presidency*, that illuminates the differences between what might be called "classical" and "contemporary" conceptions of the presidency. Tulis emphasizes the break, which he identifies particularly with Woodrow Wilson, with a relatively modest conception of the presidency. Consider for starters that prior to the twentieth century, candidates really did not engage in personal campaigns; that was viewed as beneath the dignity of the office.

---

tive Republican who might be named to the presidency under the procedures set out by the Twelfth Amendment).

2. N.Y. Const. art. XIX, § 2. Alas, they did not. The proposal for a new convention was strongly rejected.

Moreover, presidents sent written messages to Congress on the state of the Union rather than command a nationwide audience to watch them deliver an address in person before a (usually) respectful Congress. President Wilson, who (justifiably) disdained much about the U.S. Constitution, envisioned himself as a prime minister charged with truly "leading" the nation. One might, of course, also pay attention to his predecessor Teddy Roosevelt and his conception of the presidency as offering a "bully pulpit." Both, perhaps, traced their conceptions of presidential authority back to Andrew Jackson's notion that he was a "tribune of the people," by virtue of what had become de facto direct election. Perhaps not coincidentally, Jackson's opponents considered him an utter demagogue. His predecessor, John Quincy Adams, a Harvard overseer, refused to support awarding Jackson an honorary degree, writing in his diary that the university was placing its "highest literary honors upon a barbarian who could not write a sentence of grammar and could hardly spell his own name." American Indians in particular might offer yet other reasons for considering Jackson a barbarian. The point is that even by 1828 the Publian assurances set out in *The Federalist*, that the president would always be a person of unusually sterling character and civic virtue, lost their persuasiveness.

Modern communications technology, something you are far more familiar with than I, offers new possibilities to would-be demagogues. Although Calvin Coolidge, perhaps surprisingly, was the first president to make use of radio, it was of course FDR, with his fireside chats, who perfected that medium. And then there came television and, with the Obama campaigns of 2008 and 2012, the discovery of the power of social media; now we have, especially for Trump, Twitter as a device for rendering irrelevant standard forms of media as necessary agents of communicating presidents' views on matters of the day.

One might argue that the great quantum jump toward a more Caesarist conception of the presidency was the Kennedy election of 1960, when television really became important. An attractive young senator with precious little accomplishment to his name, but lots of "charisma"—a Weberian word that first made its entrance into common punditry—made it to the top of the electoral greasy pole (with due help from his family fortune and the support of Chicago mayor Richard J. Daley). He and his wife charmed the public, and his assassination made many feel that we had lost a truly incomparable leader. And, of course, there was the psychodrama of the Cuban Missile

Crisis, where Kennedy simply ignored existing political structures in favor of the Executive Committee of the National Security Council (ExComm) and, ultimately, made the decision on his own to risk World War III by ordering a "quarantine" of Cuba, which fortunately worked.

Skip forward to Ronald Reagan, who honed all of his professional skills to likewise charm the public (and, in fairness, he had demonstrated a competence for politics in governing California for eight years, even if one was, like me, appalled by his political views). In any event, we seem more and more to look to presidents for "visionary leadership," not to mention largely fictive twenty-point programs that are presented as the cures for whatever ails us. As an avid supporter of Barack Obama in 2008 (against Hillary Clinton, of course), I think it is appropriate to note the Caesarist aspects of his own remarkable campaign, including the reliance on mass rallies and vague promises.[3] Obama never once suggested that only he could guide us out of the political wilderness, but it was certainly the case that many of his supporters viewed him, in Maureen Dowd's snarky language, as "the One" whose unique abilities and "audacity" would be transformative. Not surprisingly, he disappointed such hopes, but that is another matter.

Republicans, of course, believe that Obama is increasingly governing in a Caesarist fashion. Obama has engaged in a variety of unilateral decisions, and some Republican judges agree (including, presumably, the four conservative Republicans who inhabit the current Supreme Court). I myself disagree with some of the claims to unilateral military authority that Obama has made, even if they rest on, shall we say, generous readings of congressional delegations of power to the president. Perhaps his most dramatic exercise of unilateralism was his exchange of prisoners with the Taliban in defiance of a clear congressional directive that Congress be given thirty days' notice. One can readily agree with his motives and still be a bit perturbed by his extravagant reading of his powers as commander in chief.

It is certainly the case that both Democratic and Republican presidents have been extending their powers in reaction to the breakdown of Congress as a truly functioning institution. Caesarists' power, after

---

3. Fred Lucas, "How Do Trump Crowd Sizes Really Compare to Obama's 2008 Crowds?," *The Blaze*, March 14, 2016, http://www.theblaze.com/stories/2016/03/14/how-do-trump-crowd-sizes-really-compare-to-obamas-2008-crowds/ [https://perma.cc/94XB-8PE4].

all, is not necessarily seized. It is often delegated by supine legislatures either caught up in party loyalty or a simple reluctance to engage in the hard tasks of governance (plus the burdens of having to spend an inordinate amount of time raising money in a thoroughly corrupting system of campaign finance).

What Trump wants is exactly what Weber predicted, an "acclamation" by scared masses who basically license him to do, quite literally, whatever he wishes to meet the problems he identifies. To believe, as do some of those "supporting" him without "endorsing" him (think, e.g., of Mitch McConnell), that he is capable of being internally constrained by the notion of legal obligation or duties is sheer fantasy.

So we should at least consider the frightening possibility that Weber was correct almost a century ago in suggesting that Trumpism may be a dangerous virus located in the DNA of the American constitutional order. We have seen the valorization of presidents as maximum leaders with grandiose visions, which they have "mandates" to implement, whatever it takes. No serious political system should have to contemplate the possibility of being "governed" by a narcissistic sociopath without a truly effective way—impeachment or the Twenty-Fifth Amendment really do not count—of getting rid of him until the next election four years later.

These are truly dark times, though for reasons very different from those suggested by Donald Trump. My obsessive fear is that, when[4] Hillary is elected, we will collectively congratulate ourselves for dodging a potentially fatal bullet and return to our blithe confidence. In Gerald Ford's reassuring words, "our long national nightmare is over" because "our Constitution works." I wish it were that easy. You are well aware of the important book published a few years ago by Eric Posner and Adrian Vermeule, *The Executive Unbound: After the Madisonian Republic*. It is notable for its almost exuberant embrace of much of the jurisprudential approach of Carl Schmitt, a dreadful man—he provided some of the jurisprudential scaffolding for the Nazis in the 1930s—but, nevertheless, a brilliant analyst of fundamental legal and political realities. He emphasized, for example, the development of modern political parties and the proclivity of legislators to speak to their "out-of-doors" bases rather than to engage in serious discussion and debate with their ostensible legislative colleagues. He also focused

---

4. I clearly should have written "if"!

on the importance of the rise of the modern administrative state and the inevitable discretion, in tension with certain notions of "the rule of law," exercised by administrative decision makers. Finally, he stressed the importance of "emergency" and declarations of the existence of such emergencies to understanding the modern state and the futility of adherence to established rules and laws. The central point is that perhaps the defining characteristic of the modern state is the amount of discretion it lodges in the executive branch. And, to the extent one accepts some of the more extravagant theories of the "unitary executive" as a constitutive feature of the American national government, it is the president who ultimately enjoys a remarkable degree of discretionary authority.

One might rely either on readings of the Constitution or on broad statutes passed by Congress delegating power to the executive. But either might justify the assertion that the U.S. has its own form of "constitutional dictatorship," especially dangerous if we elect a person who lacks a genuine internal compass. And, of course, the president gets to pick his own lawyers, the most important of whom are in the White House or the Office of Legal Counsel. George W. Bush found John Yoo and now-judge Jay Bybee to justify his ability to order what was in fact torture of those deemed enemies.

I have no doubt that a President Trump, empowered by the Constitution to nominate judges (who would be confirmed by a morally bankrupt Republican Party, whose members would prattle about their duty to follow the wishes of the public that elected Trump, which is how they have justified their spinelessness in endorsing Trump as their candidate), would find his share of ambitious lawyers, some educated, no doubt, at Harvard or Yale. All of this is simply to suggest that those who place their faith in the Madisonian system of checks and balances — or the virtues of attending America's elite institutions — to save us from the ravages of a sociopathic narcissist are deluding themselves. James Madison has truly, and irrevocably, left the building.

This is a bit longer than my other letters, but, then, much has happened since November. I look forward to your own take on this time of our profound discontent.

Sandy

AUGUST 7, 2016

Dear Sandy,

I do not believe that Donald Trump's rise changes the analysis of constitutional dysfunction. To the contrary, it fits perfectly into the arguments I have been making. Trump's rise was not caused by a defective Constitution, but it is a response—however mistaken—to an increasingly undemocratic and unrepublican political system. (Indeed, Trump's rhetoric plays on fears that the system is rigged against ordinary people.) At the same time, your discussion of the threats posed by Trump's candidacy highlights some of the tensions implicit in your program of constitutional reform.

Was Trump Empowered by the Hard-Wired
Constitution or by the Constitutional Order?

To what extent is Donald Trump's rise due to dysfunctional features of the Constitution? Recall the distinction I made in my first letter to you, between the "hard-wired Constitution" and the constitutional order—the entire set of rules, doctrines, and practices that structure political decision making in the United States. Your argument focuses on altering the hard-wired Constitution through amendments or a new constitutional convention. By contrast, I argue that constitutional reform should focus on features of the constitutional order.

The best explanations for Trump's rise concern our current constitutional order, but they have little to do with the hard-wired Constitution. We might divide them into three categories. The first concerns

the structure of contemporary media. The second concerns the structure of the party system. The third concerns where we are in political
time — the decline of the conservative Reagan coalition and regime,
and the gradual emergence of a new coalition and regime that will
probably (but not necessarily) be led by the Democratic Party.

A. The Structure of Mass Media

Over the past several decades, conservatives, frustrated with what
they regard as liberal bias in media and the academy, have developed
a separate set of conservative media, think tanks, and educational institutions. Coupled with the rise of talk radio, cable news, the Internet,
and geographical self-sorting, these institutions have created a conservative echo chamber. They have encouraged motivated reasoning and
helped to insulate many conservative voters from facts, opinions, and
interpretations of facts contrary to their ideology and beliefs. These
conditions primed Republican primary voters for takeover by a demagogue like Trump.

Although Trump appears to be a buffoon, he is actually extremely
skilled at media manipulation, not only of conservative media, but of
media in general. Trump knows how to use social media to speak directly to his followers, maintain audience attention, make hit-and-run
attacks on his political adversaries, and continually change the subject
when faced with the consequences of his previous controversial statements and actions.

Advertiser-driven media depend on ratings and clicks; they need
to create and extend controversies in order to compete for increasingly scarce audience attention. Recognizing this, Trump managed to
obtain disproportionate amounts of free media time during the primary season by creating a stream of entertaining and shocking controversies. In the early days of his candidacy, for example, cable news
channels carried substantial portions of his political rallies, vaulting
him into first place in the Republican primaries. All other things being
equal, voters are likely to support candidates who are most salient to
them, even when they are controversial; indeed, the more controversial a candidate, the more free airtime he or she may receive. Trump's
media savvy allowed him to leap past a crowded field and win the Republican nomination, forging a remarkably loyal following within the
Republican base.

B. The Party System

Contemporary American politics is strongly polarized and features conflict extension. Polarization means that the parties are far apart on issues with very little middle ground for compromise. Conflict extension means that the parties are polarized on more and more issues, so that if you know a politician's views on issue A, you also know their views on issue B, even if the two issues are unrelated.

Moreover, political polarization is asymmetrical. Although the Democratic Party has moved to the left in the past two decades, the Republican Party has moved much farther to the right, and its political base has become increasingly radical. Strong polarization breeds motivated reasoning, conspiracy theories, distrust of one's fellow citizens—and distrust of representative government itself. It makes people easy prey for demagogues and political con artists who promise to set everything right again.

Increasing economic inequality tends to exacerbate political polarization and enhance status anxiety. To the extent that polarization has prevented reforms that would lessen economic inequality, it creates a vicious cycle. This creates fertile ground for a politician like Trump, who thrives off division and status conflict.

Globalization and the Great Recession aggravated growing fractures within the Reagan coalition and the Republican Party. Thus, even as Republicans were increasingly polarized in opposition to liberals and Democrats, they began to fight among themselves; and different parts of the Republican coalition were increasingly at odds with each other. Although many Republican political elites, donors, and intellectuals continue to press for smaller government, entitlement reform, lower taxes for the wealthy, free trade, and immigration reform, the Republican base has developed different priorities. These include opposition to free trade and immigration, and support for social insurance programs like Medicare and Social Security, which benefit white working-class and middle-class voters.

Trump has seized on the growing fractures between Republican elites and the Republican base. He caters to the base's status anxiety and to their sense that they have repeatedly been betrayed by Republican elites and by politicians who give lip service to their values but pursue a very different agenda once in power.

C. Political Time

It is no accident that Trump's political rise occurs as the Reagan regime that dominated American politics since 1980 is breaking down, a point I alluded to in my first letter. To explain the idea of the rise and fall of political regimes in American politics, I will draw on my Yale colleague Stephen Skowronek's cyclical theory of "political time."[1] Skowronek argues that the possibilities for politics — and therefore for presidential leadership — are shaped by each president's relationship to the political regime in which he or she is elected, and by whether the regime is relatively robust or has fallen into decline.

A regime features a dominant political party that sets the tone and the agenda for politics, even if it doesn't win every election. The dominant party and the electoral coalition that keeps it in power tend to shape what seems politically possible at the time.

Political regimes rise and fall in cycles. They start out robust, even revolutionary. But as time goes on, they weaken. Their supporters split into factions and fight among themselves. New problems and demographic shifts make old agendas seem increasingly irrelevant and sap the regime's authority. The opposition party eventually adapts, pushes the dominant party off the mountaintop, starts a new regime with a new winning coalition, and the cycle of political time begins once again.

This process has happened about six times in American history, as soon as parties formed in the early republic. The first regime, led by the revolutionary party, the Federalists, lasted until 1800, when it was displaced by a new coalition led by the Jeffersonian Republicans. The Federalists eventually faded away, and for a time America had only one political party — leading to the fabled "era of good feelings." That phrase, however, disguises the increasing struggles between different factions of the Jeffersonian coalition. The coalition eventually broke down in the 1824 election, with no faction able to gain a majority, and the election was thrown into the House of Representatives. A new winning coalition formed in 1828, which marked the beginning of the Jacksonian regime. The new dominant party was the Democratic

1. Stephen Skowronek, *The Politics Presidents Make: Leadership from John Adams to Bill Clinton* (1993; repr., Harvard University Press, 2000).

Party, the first mass party, the party of the white working man as well as the party of slavery.

Tensions in the Jacksonian regime developed as defenders of slavery attempted to expand its reach to new western territories, threatening to undermine the economic interests of white working men. Both the Democrats and their major opponents, the Whigs, broke apart over slavery, leading to the American Civil War. The Republicans, the victorious party of the Union, led the next regime. Their regime was the longest-lived in American history, lasting from 1860 until the New Deal.

The corruption of the Gilded Age weakened the Republicans, who almost lost their dominant status in the 1890s, but the Democrats, led by William Jennings Bryan, blew their chance at a new populist coalition. William McKinley restructured and strengthened the Republican coalition in 1896, and the party continued to dominate until 1932, when Franklin Delano Roosevelt's election began the New Deal/civil rights regime.

The New Deal/civil rights regime lasted roughly from 1932 to 1980. The Democratic Party and its New Deal coalition were the dominant forces in politics during the period, producing (mostly) liberal and pro-union economic policies, creating modern civil rights law, and expanding the administrative and welfare states.

But as time went on, the Democrats' northern and southern wings found themselves increasingly at odds over race relations, school prayer, and what eventually became known as the "culture wars." The Republican Party regrouped and chipped away at the Democrats' dominance, and since 1980 or so we've been living in the Reagan regime, in which the Republican Party—and the conservative movement that took over the party—have set the basic terms of American politics. This is the regime of neoliberalism, deregulation, declining labor union power, and lower taxes—especially for the wealthy.

Like every regime before it, the Reagan regime has slowly been cracking up. As polarization and mutual distrust between the two major parties have become endemic, the Republican Party has become increasingly radicalized and factionalized. It has been taken over by populist demagogues and con artists, of whom Donald Trump is only the most recent example. Put in Skowronek's terminology, we are relatively late in political time—that is, we are nearing the end of the cycle of the regime's rise and fall. Republicans are momentarily united under Trump's brand of populist nativism. Even so, the party looks ripe for an electoral reckoning, if not in 2016, then in the next few election cycles.

The demographic coalition that sustained the Reagan regime has been in decline for some time and is on the verge of becoming a minority. It is gradually being supplanted by a new coalition of women, minorities, millennials, professionals, city dwellers, and college-educated people. This coalition swept Barack Obama into office and increasingly supports the Democratic Party.

The long-term shift in power between these respective coalitions was already obvious in the 2012 election; it led to the famous "autopsy" report that argued for Republicans to expand their base by supporting comprehensive immigration reform and courting the Latino vote. In a now-famous quote, a Republican operative told *National Journal*'s Ronald Brownstein that demographic changes had eclipsed traditional Republican strategies: "This is the last time anyone will try to do this"—that is, rely almost exclusively on white voters to win a presidential election.[2]

Trump, sensing an opportunity, has decided to ignore this advice, double down, and run a campaign organized around nationalism and white status anxiety. His goal is to garner an even larger percentage of white voters than Ronald Reagan, the Bushes, or Mitt Romney. He is making a calculated bet that he can revive the Reagan coalition one more time; or, more ambitiously, that he can restructure it as a coalition organized around the South, the Mountain West, and blue-collar, non-college-educated whites, especially in the Rust Belt. To do that, however, Republicans will probably have to keep their base perpetually energized. They will also have to find ways to discourage voting by the growing minority population as well as by the poor. The Republicans, in other words, will need polarization, populist outrage, and selective disenfranchisement to keep the Obama coalition from taking over.

As I explained in "The Last Days of Disco," the decline of the Republican regime and the demographic changes in the American voting population have caused the Republican Party to experience what

---

2. Ronald Brownstein, "The New Political Math," *RealClearPolitics*, August 24, 2012, http://www.realclearpolitics.com/2012/08/23/the_new_political_math_288266.html [https://perma.cc/Y977-V8DB].

we might call either a civil war or a nervous breakdown. It is precisely these circumstances that allow a demagogue like Trump to step forward, promise that he alone can make things right, and restore the former glory and status of the now-decrepit regime and its constituents. Accordingly, Trump has based his campaign on a politics of fear and status resentment, aiming his message primarily at conservative white voters, especially those who lack a college education. Trump stokes their fears about invasion from Muslim terrorists and Mexican immigrants. He appeals to their anxieties about becoming a powerless minority group and suffering a decline in their previously superior social status as whites. Trump is hardly the first Republican candidate to engage in a racially tinged status politics directed at conservative whites. But because the percentage of white voters in the population is shrinking, he has been far blunter and more overt in his appeals. He needs the votes of every white voter he can muster, and therefore he is shouting what previous candidates used to whisper.

Obviously, one can quibble about the details of these explanations for Trump's rise. But the more important point is that none of these phenomena are centrally caused by the hard-wired Constitution. To be sure, the hard-wired Constitution shapes the conditions in which parties form and party coalitions rise and fall. And because of the Electoral College, it also shapes how presidential campaigns are run. But far more important influences are structures of party competition that are not required by the hard-wired Constitution (which does not mention parties at all), as well as features of mass media that have been far more driven by technology and economics than by constitutional design.

Both you and I agree, Sandy, that structural features of our constitutional system shape presidential politics in the United States. But in explaining Trump's rise, the most important of these structural features are not hard-wired provisions of the Constitution. The most important features are part of the constitutional order; they result from statutes, administrative regulations, political conventions, the organization of political parties, and court-created constitutional doctrines that could also be modified by courts. Above all, Trump's rise is the result of economic, social, and technological factors that sit atop the incentives created by the hard-wired Constitution. If we want to prevent future demagogues like Trump, the best remedy is not an Article V amendment, much less a constitutional convention.

Presidential Caesarism

Although Trump's rise in American politics is consistent with much of the previous analysis in our exchange, it also highlights tensions in your arguments for constitutional reform.

In my previous letters, I pointed out that your program of constitutional reform seeks two different things. First, you want to make the constitutional system more democratic with a small "d." You want to eliminate unnecessary veto points and blockages in the system, and make it easier for Americans to pass laws that they need. You also want to enable ordinary individuals to circumvent elite political institutions through populist devices like the referendum and the initiative, and through constitutional conventions, which, you hope, could be staffed by ordinary individuals.

Second, you want sensible legislative solutions and progressive outcomes, with appropriate protection for civil rights and civil liberties.

In my first letter, I pointed out that these two goals are not the same and may sometimes conflict. Trump's rise as a national political candidate shows us why. On the one hand, he promises to break through existing political obstacles, reenergize government, and get things done. On the other, he promises a frightening politics that bears almost no relationship to sound public policy and threatens civil rights and civil liberties.

You advert to the problem in your discussion of Max Weber and his suggestion that "all systems of 'direct election by the people of the bearer of supreme power' have within them an impulse . . . toward Caesarism." You argue that Weber's logic applies increasingly to the United States.

There is a little bit of irony in your invocation of Weber. You have argued that the central problem with our system of government is that it is insufficiently parliamentary and insufficiently responsive to popular will. You want to break down the barriers that constrain majorities. Yet the system that you want to move toward is the system that Weber thought contained the seeds of Caesarism!

Moreover, if your fear is demagogues and dictators, the last things you should be pushing for are national referenda and initiatives. History has shown repeatedly that when demagogues and dictators seek to consolidate power, they turn to direct democracy to evade constitutional limitations and demonstrate that they enjoy the support of the people. One can easily imagine Donald Trump turning to direct democracy to circumvent a polarized Congress and justify one of his outrageous schemes.

I think that there is a better way to make your point. The framers of our Constitution created a system of checks and balances to prevent demagogues and dictators from seizing power, and from working their will if they did gain power. These checks and balances also distinguish American democracy from a parliamentary system. You point out, however, that this system of checks and balances has gradually been undermined, especially in foreign affairs, but also through the expansion of the administrative state. (This is what you mean when you say that James Madison has left the building.) Moreover, because of partisan polarization and gridlock, presidents have increasingly turned to the administrative state to create the effective equivalent of presidential lawmaking. The worse that congressional gridlock becomes, the more presidents will push the envelope of what they can do within the executive branch (including through waivers and agreements with individual states and localities). Doing an end run around Congress infuriates the president's opponents in Congress even more. They refuse to cooperate, double down on their intransigence, and the cycle continues. To be sure, as you and I have argued in our work on constitutional dictatorship, there are limits to presidential unilateralism, especially in domestic affairs. But that does not keep frustrated presidents from testing those limits.

The result is a system that has many of the dangers of parliamentarianism with none of its benefits. Increasingly, Congress fails to be a serious partner in governing, while the president grows ever more powerful and ever more crucial to solve the nation's problems. Indeed, in the public's eyes, the president becomes virtually the sole cause of the country's successes and misfortunes. You and I have written about America's gradual movement toward a plebiscitary presidency, in which the president asserts that he or she can lead the country out of its current problems and into a glorious future. In a plebiscitary presidency, media manipulation becomes increasingly important. Voters pay less attention to substantive issues (to the extent that they ever did) and more attention to personal charisma, emotional connection, and grand narratives about the country's direction. Plebiscitary presidencies also encourage unscrupulous candidates to engage in status politics, pitting social groups against each other and manipulating people's fears about potential loss of status. Because, at least in the short run, social status is a zero-sum good, status politics can make politics more emotional, volatile, and subject to motivated reasoning. Moreover, reforms to the system of presidential primaries adopted by both parties in the early 1970s have made presidential nominations depend much more on the vote of the most politically mobilized and ideological segments of the general public. Primary voters—especially ideologically extreme voters, anxious about their social status, and seeking reassurance and emotional uplift—may be the most vulnerable to the blandishments and manipulations of a demagogue like Trump.

People on both sides of the political divide understand the dangers, although they describe them in different ways. Recently, political conservatives, who had previously advocated for a powerful and "unitary" executive, have begun to express great discomfort with the administrative state. Part of this is due to the fact that conservatives fear that they will not control the executive branch very often in the near future. But part of it is also due to principled concerns about long-term threats to representative democracy and to the rule of law.

In the face of these criticisms, liberals should resist the temptation—almost automatic in today's polarized politics—to engage in reflexive defense of the status quo. Rather, they should take the critique of the administrative state seriously. In the face of congressional obstruction, presidents may have expanded their lawmaking capacities within the administrative state for lack of any better alternatives. But doing so has generated a vicious cycle—the more presidents try to solve problems unilaterally, the more intransigent Congress becomes. And in the process, this strategy has distorted the system of checks and balances that guards against abuses by demagogues and would-be dictators. Liberals should be eager to find ways to remedy these distortions as we move to a less polarized politics—for they will not always be in control of the executive branch either.

Although we differ on the causes, you and I agree that our current political practices are unsustainable in the long run, and that they create two serious dangers. The first is that the country will be unable to deal effectively with the long-term problems it faces and the various crises that may confront it from time to time.

The second problem is that if our system of governance is not reformed, it will increasingly fail to protect important civil rights and civil liberties. (In saying this, I do not pretend that it currently protects them adequately.) The dispute between us is not whether constitutional reform is necessary. It is about what kind of constitutional reform makes the most sense.

Many of our current problems, but by no means all, will be ameliorated as we gradually transition from the decaying Reagan regime into a new one, whether that new regime turns out to be dominated by Republicans or Democrats. Then we must begin the long, slow process of making our political system both more democratic and more republican.

Such a transition will be necessary for any kind of serious constitutional reform to occur. In fact, the kind of constitutional reforms you seek—Article V amendments or a new constitutional convention—are nonstarters in our currently polarized politics. In any case, my hope is that the transition to a new regime will offer possibilities for reform of the constitutional order that do not require Article V amendment or a new convention—although, as I noted previously, I am not opposed to either in principle.

An important part of the solution, therefore, is to maintain constitutional faith and allow American politics time to transition, even as we continue to press for reforms. I advocate patience but not quiescence. We may not be able to do much in the short term to fix our broken politics—other than trying to hasten the transition through winning elections. But that is hardly a reason to refrain from pointing out the many flaws in our political system and persuading people why we need to make changes. When reform finally becomes possible, we will need the best possible proposals for how to proceed.

Jack

NOVEMBER 26, 2016

Dear Jack,

So our epistolary exchange continues, unexpectedly, for a very simple reason. The barely imaginable in fact happened. To paraphrase Abraham Lincoln, "we are now engaged in a great natural experiment to see if the vision of a Republican Form of Government enunciated in 1776 and then again in 1787 will endure," or if we are condemned to suffer the fate of most such experiments and decline into one or another form of authoritarian rule.

The primary constitutional problem presented by Donald Trump, I think we both agree, is that the American constitutional order, that blend of written institutional structures and unwritten conventions and political culture, is supposed to prevent the takeover of our political system by an unscrupulous demagogue without the slightest qualification to be president. They failed, largely, I believe, for the reasons you outline; Trump realized better than did any other candidate that the traditional media have become delegitimized by the rise of social media that privileges "truthiness" and, indeed, outright lies over what used to be regarded as facts. Similarly, he recognized how the Republican Party had become vulnerable to a hostile takeover.

I would, however, continue to assign the deficiencies of the 1787 Constitution at least a bit of causal influence in explaining the sheer level of rage at the breakdown of ordinary governance that presumably motivated some of the Trump voters to believe they had "nothing to lose" in rejecting what would almost undoubtedly have turned into four more years of the ineffectual and infuriating status quo, given

the continuation of divided and gridlocked national government. As I
wrote above, I believe that the pleasure of a Clinton election, even if
accompanied by a Democratic Senate (and thus the recapture of the
Supreme Court), would have been succeeded quickly by depressed
recognition that Paul Ryan and the Freedom Caucus would allow her
no domestic victories and that she would, in 2020, be the most vulnerable incumbent at least since Herbert Hoover in 1932. Now we might
hope that that fate is assigned to Donald Trump!

But I worry about getting to 2020. I do think that we are in the
most serious existential internal crisis since 1860. Significantly more
Americans preferred Hillary Clinton than Donald Trump, but our
completely anachronistic Electoral College tossed the election to the
second-place finisher. No sane political system would adopt such a
decision procedure today. The Electoral College, like the Senate, is a
bizarre affirmative action program that overweighs the voting power
of small states and the political power of those lucky residents of battleground states. The states where most Americans live—think only of
California, Texas, New York, and Illinois—received almost no visits or
genuine consideration from the candidates. More to the point, most of
those who opposed Donald Trump consider him an illegitimate president on both procedural and substantive grounds. As to the first, he
ran the most completely dishonest campaign in American history. He
is a congenital liar who was more than willing to repeat whatever he
thought might gain him the votes of basically ignorant people who
made no effort to check the accuracy of his statements or, even worse,
simply didn't care that they were lies. When one adds to the elemen-
tal dishonesty of the campaign the systematic efforts to suppress the
vote in such Republican bastions as Wisconsin and North Carolina, for
starters, then one has additional reason to doubt the integrity of the
overall process, even without taking into consideration the inanity of
the Electoral College. But there is also the fact that Donald Trump is
totally without any of the intellectual skills or personal virtues that we
look for in presidents. If he is to be obeyed and taken seriously as president, it is for the reason set out in *King Lear*: Even "a dog's obeyed in
office."

All of this helps to explain why I, and many others, joined, post-
election, in pleading with Republican electors to save the republic by
acting under the original vision of the Electoral College, i.e., to engage
in what Publius in *Federalist* No. 1 called "reflection and choice" as to

who should take the national helm rather than simply act like lemmings committed to a potentially suicidal choice for the nation. Two UT colleagues and I published an op-ed in the *New York Daily News* endorsing the proposition that electors should exercise their constitutional right (and duty) to engage in autonomous choice regarding who should be the next president of the United States. "They can try and steal it from President Elect Trump," wrote an angry respondent, "but if they do get ready for Martial Law under Obama because there are 70 million of us and we'll make the radical left wing riots currently underway look like a picnic. The Establishment lost this one, deal with it." Keith Whittington, when visiting UT for an event shortly after the inauguration, agreed that depriving Trump of the presidency might have triggered civil war. It is difficult to disagree with this analysis (and diagnosis).

In any event, I do believe that, at least psychologically, we are at the brink of civil war inasmuch as critical masses on both right and left basically look at their fellow Americans as enemies who must be stopped at almost any cost. This, to put it mildly, is not ordinary politics. It represents the breakdown of a functioning political system that relies on a certain code of what might be described as a willingness to be a "good sport" after losing an election and saying, as did the fans first of the Brooklyn Dodgers and then the Chicago Cubs, "wait till next year"—and "next year" finally came for both teams, of course. Is that a good enough reason to roll over and accept the verdict of the minority of the American voters who voted for Trump and nonetheless won because of the Electoral College? It all depends on how dangerous one believes that Trump and his minions are, and I believe they are dangerous indeed.

Perhaps this is all too melodramatic, even apocalyptic. President Obama himself has apparently reassured his own daughters that this, too, will pass, that America is too resilient to be permanently deflected from moving further along the arc of justice. I obviously hope he is right. Donald Trump, after all, seems primarily to be rapaciously devoted to amassing greater and greater wealth, and he clearly views the presidency as a path to enhanced fame and fortune. New American wars, and especially a world war, would not be conducive to his financial gain. In the meantime, concerned Democrats must do everything they can to identify and work with those honorable Republicans who actually meant "never Trump." If there are only half a dozen in the

Senate, then Trump's worst appointments (or at least those requiring Senate confirmation) can be blocked. Undoubtedly this will mean
that Democrats themselves will have to acquiesce in some conservative programs they would ordinarily do everything in their power to
oppose. That, for better or worse, is what serious compromise entails.
The original Constitution came into being only because its proponents
were willing to compromise with slave-owning states (thorough the
three-fifths rule, most notably) and small states (through equal voting
power in the Senate).

One can make a serious argument that the Constitution wasn't
worth it, especially since we now live every single day with the consequences of both of those compromises. But perhaps it was. There
are times when pacts with the devil are necessary, as with the alliance with Joseph Stalin against Adolf Hitler. Nothing that Al Qaeda
could do so threatens the American fabric as does Donald Trump and
the truly deplorable part of his base, even if we take necessary care to
concede that they may represent only a relatively small subset of the
larger number of people who voted for Trump in their understandable
desire to remonstrate (a true euphemism) against elites of both parties
who had almost willfully ignored their plight in the rush toward globalization. No doubt many of those who voted for the Nazis in 1933 also
had "understandable reasons" to do so. It really didn't matter once the
Nazis seized power through legal means.

Please persuade me that I'm wrong to be so anxious about our
country and its future under a Trump presidency.

Your devoted friend,

Sandy

DECEMBER 3, 2016

Dear Sandy,

We began this exchange over a year ago by asking whether American democracy has become dysfunctional. Along the way, we have debated what "dysfunction" means, and whether the causes of dysfunction lie in our Constitution or in other aspects of our political system. We have also debated whether the causes of dysfunction are hardwired—requiring an Article V amendment or convention to repair—or whether the solutions lie in some combination of political reform, mobilization, perseverance, and persistence.

The 2016 election has confirmed that American democracy is dysfunctional. But it has confirmed it in a most unexpected way. Both of us assumed that Hillary Clinton would win the presidency and that we would face four years of political gridlock and trench warfare. What has happened instead is that Americans have elected a demagogue to the presidency.

The Fragility of Republics

The founders, steeped in the history of the rise and fall of republics, worried that something like this could and would come to pass. Republics, they believed, are delicately calibrated instruments of political power that require perpetual vigilance and civic virtue to maintain. Civic virtue means devotion to the public good and the ability and the willingness to sacrifice short-term political self-interest for the greater good of the res publica—the public thing that simultaneously constitutes and motivates a well-ordered state.

The famous quip, attributed to Benjamin Franklin, that the framers had founded "a republic, . . . if you can keep it,"[1] adverted to the history of the rise and fall of republics and the difficulty of maintaining them over long periods of time. Speaking at the conclusion of the 1787 Convention, Franklin predicted that the new government "is likely to be well administered for a course of years, and can only end in Despotism, as other forms have done before it, when the people shall become so corrupted as to need despotic Government, being incapable of any other."[2]

Why are republics difficult to keep? Republics are always subject to corruption: corruption of civic officials, who seek to promote their own interests and entrench themselves in power; and corruption of the citizens, who become cynical, internally divided, and lose faith in the idea of a common good and in the possibility of a common project of governance involving their fellow citizens.

The corruption of republics involves more than dishonesty and selfishness. Above all, it involves a loss of faith—faith in the ability and the goodwill of leaders and public institutions, and faith in the goodwill of one's fellow citizens. Loss of faith and selfishness go together—the one exacerbates the other. In a republic sliding into corruption, citizens look around them and all they see are smug, dishonest elites, scheming politicians, condescending cosmopolitans, and baskets of deplorables. Because the people have lost faith in public institutions, in their fellow citizens, in the possibility of working for common ends—indeed, in the very idea of achieving a common good—they become selfish, clannish, angry, suspicious, despairing, and distrustful. Their attitudes and actions further corrode faith in public institutions and in the republic, and the cycle of corruption continues.

In the traditional account, as republics decay into ever greater corruption, the public hungers for strong leadership to repair what has fallen into disrepair. Their desire to set things right encourages the rise of unscrupulous demagogues, who offer blandishments and lies;

1. Walter Isaacson, *Benjamin Franklin: An American Life* (Simon & Schuster, 2003), 459.
2. *The Records of the Federal Convention of 1787*, rev. ed., ed. Max Farrand (Yale University Press, 1966), 641 (September 17, 1787).

they promise that they will restore the republic's lost glory through the sheer force of their will.

Demagogues do not usually sneak up unawares. Members of the public often know that demagogues are selfish, unethical, and unscrupulous, but they convince themselves that turning to such leaders is the only way to smash corrupt institutions and solve the country's problems. Once in power, however, demagogues become tyrants, bringing republican government to an end.

This is the traditional story of how republics decay and fall. The story was well known to the founders of our country. They hoped that they could create a new kind of republic that would resist the natural tendencies toward decay in all republics throughout history. The devices they hoped would prevent this fate included a large federal republic that would diffuse and temper factionalism, as well as federalism, separation of powers, checks and balances, and institutions of civil society that would inculcate virtue in the citizenry and instill respect for education, learning, and accomplishment.

How well does the traditional account of the decay of republics match our present situation? The resemblance is altogether frightening. Republican themes have been implicit in our entire exchange of letters about democracy and dysfunction. Government dysfunction has caused—and been caused by—political polarization, factionalism, the corruption of the political process, and the public's loss of faith in public institutions and in the public good. Decades of politicians exacerbating political polarization for short-term political gain, elite arrogance, institutional failure, and loss of public faith have spewed forth a demagogue whose populist appeals, brash personality, and dishonest tactics almost perfectly fit the classical description. Not only has the demagogue taken over one of the two major political parties, but he has actually won the presidency.

The framers knew that corruption comes to republics both from within and from without. They understood that foreign powers would be happy to sow confusion and disorder within a republic to benefit their interests. This fear has also been realized in 2016. Amazing as it seems, there is evidence that the Russian government engaged in a systematic disinformation campaign to confuse and mislead the American electorate, and to help to throw the election to Donald Trump, widely thought to be more pro-Russian than Hillary Clinton.

In short, democratic dysfunction, and what the founders would have called republican corruption, has brought forth a demagogue. According to the familiar story, the next step is that the demagogue becomes a tyrant, and the tyrant ends republican government.

Is that how the story continues?

Republican Fail-Safes and Republican Insurance

You fear the worst, Sandy, and raise the specter of secession and civil war. I do not argue that the prospects for American democracy are particularly bright in the near term. But the familiar story of the decline and fall of republics is not destined to be our fate, at least not yet.

Remember that the American Constitution—the very constitution that you have so eloquently criticized—is not simply a set of procedures for self-governance. Our Constitution was also designed to be a device for resisting demagogues. It trades off the best possible system of democratic governance in order to avoid the worst.

A constitution is designed to make politics possible. It is designed to make people engage in politics rather than have the struggle for power degenerate into anarchy, dictatorship, or violence. A well-designed republican constitution, accordingly, is designed to make republics possible, and to keep them operating as republics over time, despite the multiple temptations and corruptions that republics historically suffer. Such a constitution may be awkward in many respects. But that is acceptable if the awkwardness buys insurance against republican corruption—because that corruption, unchecked, leads to tyranny, anarchy, and civil war.

This point about constitutional structures as insurance against demagogues is the converse of an argument you have often made about the undemocratic defects of our constitutional system. You point out that there are several features of the Constitution that may not cause serious problems in the ordinary course of affairs. Yet, as you have often reminded me, building a house on a hundred-year floodplain involves the risk that, every hundred years or so, there will be a flood that will destroy your property. In the same way, you point out that, every now and then, undemocratic features of the Constitution may seriously frustrate democratic will. This risk motivates your argument for reforming our constitutional system to get rid of its inefficient and undemocratic features.

But the flip side of this argument is that certain features of a constitution may not merely be kludges or inefficient compromises that
undermine democracy. Rather, they may trade off democratic efficiency in the ordinary course of affairs for political fail-safes. Such political fail-safes keep the struggle for power within republican politics
rather than spinning out of control into tyranny and civil war.

These features of our constitutional system are often described as
slowing down politics and making change more difficult. But many
of these features do more than simply block precipitous action; they
also give many different people and groups a stake in governance so
that they have reason to continue to work within the political constitution rather than outside it. These fail-safes are a kind of republican
insurance. They act as checks on situations that may only rarely come
to pass, but they serve as security for moments when, to borrow your
metaphor, great political floods threaten to overwhelm the entire republic.

You might think of a well-designed constitution like a well-designed
cybersecurity system. A computer system connected to the Internet
is constantly being bombarded by various kinds of cyber-attacks.
Viruses and worms are always trying to infect it. Social engineers—
that is, con artists and tricksters—are always trying to hack the system
through ruses and tricks. (Apparently this is how the DNC and John
Podesta's e-mails were hacked.) A good security system—there is no
perfect system—tries to ward off these constant attacks as best it can,
and it inevitably trades off other goods in order to achieve a decent
modicum of security.

Like most well-designed security systems, a good system for defending republican government does not have a single door with a
single lock to be picked. Rather it has multiple layers and perimeters
of defense. Some of these defenses are hard-wired into the constitutional text, while others, although not hard-wired, are part of what
you call the Constitution of Settlement. Many, if not most of them,
make the system more undemocratic in your terms. Yet, to continue
the metaphor of computer security, what you have described as bugs
in the American constitutional system can also be understood as features.

Some of the defenses in our constitutional system prevent demagogues from ever achieving political prominence. Others prevent
them from being placed on the ballot as candidates in a general elec-

tion. Others keep them from being elected. And still others limit what demagogues can do once they achieve office.

Several of these constitutional defenses, designed to prevent demagogues from ever gaining power, have already fallen in the course of the 2016 election. But others do not kick in until the demagogue becomes president. The question we now face is whether these remaining defenses will hold. There is still hope. And if we get to the 2020 and 2024 elections intact, with checks and balances, with functioning courts, with a smooth rotation of political power, in which the losers leave office peacefully and the winners don't exact revenge on them, our system will have proved robust as a constitution against demagogues. Don't get me wrong: a great deal may have been lost or damaged in the process, but the republic will have survived. In situations like the present, one has to scale back one's ambitions and defend the core of the constitutional project.

One of the ironies of our exchange as it has developed over the course of a year is that you find yourself arguing for the use of one of these fail-safes, these defenses of republican government. Neither of us likes the Electoral College, and you have identified it as a key example of what is undemocratic about our Constitution. In 2006, for example, you wrote that "the Electoral College . . . supplies the decisive and overriding reason for rejecting the status quo and supporting a convention entitled to propose significant revisions. It is an undemocratic and perverse part of the American system of government that ill serves the United States." Nevertheless, in today's desperate circumstances, you argue that public-spirited individuals and groups should push for members of the Electoral College to support someone other than Donald Trump on December 19th. Consistent with the republican tradition of devotion to the common good, you argue that liberals and Democrats should put aside their short-term self-interest and get behind a consensus candidate from the Republican Party, because that is the best way to ensure that the nation will accept the legitimacy of the result.

Denying Trump an Electoral College majority, in turn, would throw the presidential election into the House of Representatives, in which each state delegation would have one vote. California and Wyoming would have an equal say in who becomes our next president—a system of voting every bit as undemocratic as the malapportioned Senate. Your hope is that the House would pick an alternative to Trump—

even someone who had never faced the voters in 2016. In 2006, you stated your staunch opposition to this particular feature of our Constitution; indeed, you called it "a national constitutional crisis just waiting to happen."

In ordinary times—indeed, as recently as a year ago—you would have pointed to the Electoral College and the House's power to choose the president as some of the worst features of our Constitution because they are so deeply in conflict with democratic norms. But, as you have pointed out, these are not ordinary times. And the argument in your last letter makes the case for the importance of republican fail-safes in a democratic constitution.

Even so, I am skeptical about your particular solution. The Electoral College and the House of Representatives might have helped to preserve republican government in the early 1800s. After all, in the election of 1800, they eventually gave us Thomas Jefferson rather than Aaron Burr. But it is less likely that they will have the same effect in 2016. Neither the Electoral College nor the House of Representatives offers a very significant chance of preventing Trump's election. The solution you propose requires a great deal of coordination among strangers, and it requires that the Republican Party quickly converge on a consensus candidate in opposition to Trump, something the party was conspicuously unable to do throughout the Republican primary process.

Beyond the Electoral College, however, lie many other fail-safes in our constitutional system. Most of them form part of the Constitution of Settlement; some of them are hard-wired into the Constitution and would require an Article V amendment to change. You would probably regard almost all of them as either undemocratic or as unduly limiting the ability of "We the People" to act expeditiously to realize their will.

Republican Defense

What are these remaining defenses? They include the staggered system of elections for president, Senate, and House; the requirements of bicameralism and presentment; the internal rules of the Senate and House, the filibuster, and the various limitations on the use of the reconciliation procedure to get around the filibuster.

Other defenses arise from our federal system: separate state governments with multiple offices that answer to different constituencies than the federal government, and the practical necessity of power sharing between federal and state governments in a host of federal programs. These practical features of federalism are far more important to the preservation of republican government than the entire history of judicial attempts at protecting state sovereignty or imposing dual federalism. They protect republicanism by continuously generating a cadre of opponents to contest the dominant regime, and by giving these opponents a stake in engaging in politics from within the system rather than outside of it. As long as the opposition party can exert influence in state and local government, it is never fully shut out of politics. It can live to fight another day. Indeed, the party system often operates counter-cyclically: as one party dominates the presidency, the other often makes gains in Congress, and especially in state and local governments.

When Trump takes office in January 2017, Republicans will control both houses of Congress and most state legislatures. But a regular system of staggered elections—every two years for the House, every four for the president, and every six for the Senate—is hard-wired into the Constitution. This distinguishes our presidential system from the sort of parliamentary systems you favor. It guarantees that it is very difficult for one party to hold on to all of the levers of power for an extended period of time. It makes revolutionary change difficult, unless the people keep returning the same party to power over and over again.

The staggered system of elections is the Constitution's most overlooked weapon against the rise of dictatorship. A staggered system of elections helps ensure that the opposition party has a chance to control at least some levers of power.

Generally speaking, the president's party usually loses seats in Congress during the midterm elections. If President Trump proves incompetent or unpopular, he may well lose control of one or both houses of Congress by 2018. Losing even one house makes it possible for the Democrats to serve as a check on executive misbehavior through congressional committee investigations. Because of our hyper-polarized politics, whenever Congress and the president are from the same party, Congress engages in relatively little oversight of the president. Divided government thus offers a check on corruption and malfeasance, and gives the opposition party a platform to make its case.

Even if the Democrats don't win control of one house of Congress—because of gerrymandered House districts and the large number of Senate seats Democrats must defend in 2018—the Democrats might still gain enough seats to make it difficult for Republicans to pass legislation through Republican votes alone. At that point, many of Trump's most dangerous plans will be off the table.

Conversely, if the Republicans' midterm losses are especially significant, and if Trump is blamed for them, a further check arises. Trump may face a serious primary challenge within his own party. When this happens (as it did, for example, in 1968, 1980, and 1992), it strongly undermines an incumbent's chances for reelection. Most incumbent presidents are strong enough to prevent serious primary challenges. If one or more plausible candidates rise to challenge Trump in the 2020 Republican primaries, it will signify that important elements of his party are willing to stand up to him.

The 2018 and 2020 elections are also important because they will determine who draws the redistricting maps for both state and federal elections in the next decade. Republicans leveraged their successes in the 2010 election to lock in a partisan advantage both in state legislatures and in the House of Representatives. Democrats have a chance to undo some of those advantages in the next decade.

These structural defenses can't prevent everything, of course. As you and I have written in our work on constitutional dictatorship, over the years Congress has delegated so much control to the White House that in many aspects of domestic and foreign policy, the president can act unilaterally. The sad fact is that Trump doesn't need to innovate all that much to cause a great deal of damage to our national interests—he can rely on the techniques that previous presidents have developed. Many of these techniques were developed by presidents who faced increasing gridlock, government inertia, and congressional irresponsibility. But tools crafted with the best of intentions can still be abused by later presidents. We can only guess at what Trump will do with the quasi-dictatorial powers of the modern presidency. (At the same time, executive overreach will open up another potential site of resistance—through judicial review of the administrative state.)

And then there is the elephant in the room: the possibility of another terrorist attack on American soil. Unlike George W. Bush, Trump might be blamed for it, further diminishing his ability to govern effectively. But it is also possible that he will use the attack as an opportunity to expand the powers of the president and limit civil liberties. He will rally his supporters, find his scapegoats, and demand the power to act quickly and effectively. He will confuse energy and initiative with cruelty and self-aggrandizement, as demagogues so often do.

How to Defeat a Demagogue

There are no guarantees, but the system of staggered elections is among the most important defenses the American Constitution presents to demagogic ambitions. In a parliamentary system, one might hope to generate a vote of no confidence and cause the leader's government to fall. But in the American system, the most important thing one can do to counter a demagogue is to win successive elections at both the state and federal level.

Complaining that Trump is arrogant, ignorant, uncouth, and corrupt is not the most likely means of winning those elections. Trump's supporters already know that he is arrogant, ignorant, uncouth, and corrupt, but they voted for him anyway. They supported him because they wanted dramatic change that would make their lives better. Some of the people who voted for him didn't like him at all, but merely regarded him as the lesser of two evils; they hoped against their better judgment that he could change things for the better.

Understanding all this is the key to the proper political strategy. The way to defeat Trump is not to reveal him as a vulgarian, or even as corrupt or self-dealing, but to fight him on the questions of change and reform. His power is his promise of change. Explode the promise and his magic dissipates.

It is not enough to show that Trump is a hypocrite—one must show that he is an *ineffective* hypocrite. Demonstrate that his promises of change are illusory, and that his policies hurt the very people who support him. Show that he has not drained the swamp of corruption but only made things worse. Make people want to give the other party a chance, just as they have done so many times before. This was the sword that Trump wielded against Hillary Clinton; and it is the weapon that might be wielded against Trump. Trump enters the White House without a popular majority and with some of the lowest net favorability ratings of any first-term president in recent American history. A majority of the public is already skeptical of him and may turn on him if he cannot quickly bring significant reform to an increasingly restless America.

The credibility of a demagogue like Trump stems from his promise to shake up the lethargy of government, to bring change, and to improve people's lives. The source of his power is also the source of his greatest vulnerability. To defeat him, one must bog him down, divert him, frustrate him, waste his energies.

A Demagogue in Political Time

In my previous letters, I've argued for understanding our political situation in terms of what Stephen Skowronek calls political time—where we are in the cycle of the rise and fall of political regimes led by dominant parties and supported by dominant coalitions. Skowronek's central argument is that the rise and fall of regimes not only affects the agendas of politics, but also affects presidents' opportunities for successful leadership. So if we want to predict whether Trump will prove to be a successful demagogue or a failure, we have to think about where he fits in political time. And this analysis gives me some hope that, although we are in for a very rough period, Trump will ultimately not succeed.

Newly elected presidents have one of four possible relationships to the existing regime. The new president can be affiliated with the dominant party or opposed to it. And the president can take office when the regime is still robust or when it is vulnerable to being overthrown.

Reconstructive presidents—such as Andrew Jackson, Abraham Lincoln, Franklin D. Roosevelt, and Ronald Reagan—begin as oppositional leaders when the existing regime is weak; they successfully topple it and start a new one. The presidents of their party who follow them (for example, Martin Van Buren, Ulysses S. Grant, Harry S. Truman, and George H. W. Bush) are *affiliated* with the now-dominant regime while it is still strong. They try to keep its factions united and its commitments going through changing times.

Next are presidents from the opposition party who take office when the regime they oppose is still robust. Skowronek calls these leaders *preemptive* presidents, because they try to preempt the dominant party's politics by triangulating, borrowing ideas from the dominant party, and seeking a "Third Way." These presidents include Grover Cleveland, Woodrow Wilson, Richard Nixon, Bill Clinton, and (it now appears) Barack Obama. They are oppositional leaders who are unable to fundamentally change the politics of their era, so they have to learn to live within it. Because they are swimming against the political tides, their authority and their political legitimacy are always in question; the dominant party throws everything it can at them, trying to destroy them. Even so, if these presidents learn to compromise and make the most of their limited opportunities, they can be quite successful. The tacking and weaving of preemptive presidents often infuriates partisans on both sides. The other party denounces them as unscrupulous, criminal, and illegitimate; members of their own party often deride them as sellouts.

In the fourth category are presidents who are allied with the regime but who take office when the regime is debilitated. Examples are John Quincy Adams, James Buchanan, Herbert Hoover, and Jimmy Carter. They have the misfortune to lead the dominant party when the regime is losing its legitimacy and the party's factions are at each other's throats. They try to revive the coalition by adjusting the regime's commitments to changing circumstances—Carter's embrace of deregulation is a good example—but they lack the necessary political skill to make the transition and are simply not up to the task. Skowronek calls them *disjunctive* presidents because things tend to fall apart on their watch, leading to a new reconstructive presidency.

Let's think about Trump's opportunities for success in these terms. Is he likely to be a reconstructive, affiliated, preemptive, or disjunctive president?

Trump takes office at the end of the Reagan regime; he enters the White House when his party's coalition is weak and factionalized. Therefore, I believe that he is primed for what Skowronek calls "the politics of disjunction," in which a president allied with an aging political regime promises to restore its dominance and former greatness, is unable to keep all of the elements of his coalition together, and as a result presides over the regime's dissolution. Disjunctive presidencies are usually failures; the opposition party successfully repudiates them, producing a new and robust political regime to replace them.

There are good reasons to believe that Trump will be a disjunctive president, bringing the Reagan era to a close.[3] He fits many features of

3. Julia Azari and Corey Robin, among others, have reached a similar conclusion. See Julia Azari, "Trump's Presidency Signals the End of the Reagan Era," *VOX*, December 1, 2016, https://www.vox.com/mischiefs-of-faction/2016/12/1/13794680/trump -presidency-reagan-era-end; Corey Robin, "The Politics Trump Makes," *n+1*, January 11, 2017, https://nplusonemag.com/online-only/online-only/the-politics-trump-makes/.

the ideal type. For example, although nominally affiliated with a decaying regime, "the actions these presidents take on their own behalf are as disruptive to the status quo as any."[4] Indeed, Skowronek notes, "one of the great ironies of the politics of disjunction is that the presidents who come to office in these sorts of situations tend to have only the most tenuous relationship to the establishments they represent." "Long-festering problems within the regime" tend to produce leaders "only nominally affiliated with it." In trying to fix the country's problems, they "often press major departures of their own from the standard formulas and priorities set in the old agenda."[5] (Trump's policies on trade, immigration, and foreign alliances immediately come to mind.)

As differences within the coalition become increasingly obvious and difficult to manage, disjunctive candidates argue that they are able to fix things because they have special technical abilities. For example, they might portray themselves as extremely skilled diplomats and politicians (John Quincy Adams, James Buchanan), outstanding technocrats and problem solvers (Herbert Hoover, Jimmy Carter); or, as in Trump's case, outstanding deal makers. They explain to the public that what is important is not ideological purity but the ability to fix what is broken and to get things done.

In like fashion, Trump has used his image as a successful businessman who is good at making deals to assuage different parts of the Republican coalition. "Nobody knows the system better than me, which is why I alone can fix it," Trump famously announced when he accepted his party's nomination at the Republican National Convention.

Stephen Skowronek's interview in *The Nation* suggests that Trump fits the disjunctive ideal type far better than that of a reconstructive president. Richard Kreitner, "What Time Is It? Here's What the 2016 Election Tells Us about Obama, Trump, and What Comes Next," *The Nation*, November 22, 2016, https://www.thenation.com/article /what-time-is-it-heres-what-the-2016-election-tells-us-about-obama-trump-and -what-comes-next/. See also Thomas M. Keck, "Is President Trump More Like Viktor Orbán or Franklin Pierce?, SSRN, February 28, 2018, https://papers.ssrn.com/sol3 /papers.cfm?abstract_id=2950015. Scott Lemieux, by contrast, argues that Trump symbolizes "a new period of competition between increasingly polarized parties." Scott Lemieux, "Is Donald Trump the Next Jimmy Carter?," *The New Republic*, January 23, 2017, at https://newrepublic.com/article/140041/donald-trump-next-jimmy -carter.

4. Stephen Skowronek, *The Politics Presidents Make: Leadership from John Adams to Bill Clinton* (repr., Harvard University Press, 2000), 40.

5. Skowronek, *The Politics Presidents Make*, 40.

As Skowronek puts it, in the last days of a regime, mastery of technique—in this case deal making and business acumen—"is a hallmark of the politics of disjunction."[6] Focusing on technique allows the new president to remain ambiguous about what he or she stands for. This allows each side of the coalition to believe that it will get what it wants from the new presidency.

Unfortunately, the politics of disjunction presents a gauntlet that is close to impossible to traverse successfully. Disjunctive presidents are caught between the demands of increasingly antagonistic factions, whom they cannot all please simultaneously. Technique is not enough to keep the coalition together or maintain its legitimacy. Being a great deal maker, for example, is not enough if people don't like the deals, or if they come to believe that you have sold them out. Eventually such presidents discover they cannot maintain public support; they are undone by internal divisions within their own party, resistance from the opposition party, and the unexpected calamities that befall every presidency.

There are no guarantees that Trump will fit into a predetermined ideal type. He has confounded expectations many times before. Nevertheless, our best hope is to act on these assumptions about where we stand in political time. History will not take care of itself; these kinds of leaders fail because people actively oppose them. They fail because their political coalition begins weakened and falls apart in the face of constant political opposition. If Trump's political coalition is fractious, one must prevent it from coalescing and regaining strength. One must work continuously to split his coalition, by highlighting the choices that divide congressional Republicans, by finding common ground with conservative Never Trumpers, and by peeling off people who only viewed Trump as the lesser of two evils.

The Upside of Dysfunction

Above all, to defeat a demagogue whose power comes from the promise of change, one must make change difficult and impede the smooth progress of his administration's ambitions. In constitutional terms, one must use all of the tools in the American constitutional system to hinder, delay, and frustrate his efforts. To defeat a demagogue like

6. Skowronek, *The Politics Presidents Make*, 40.

Trump, in other words, one must use the tools that you, Sandy, have repeatedly denounced as making our Constitution undemocratic. In a period of abnormal politics, our goal is not a frictionless path for official action; instead, we must defend the republic.

This brings our discussion full circle, back to the issues that began our debate. Without defending all of the undemocratic features of our constitutional system, let me suggest that at least some of them serve as crucial insurance for republicanism. The next few years will demonstrate their value, and your proposals to eliminate or displace them are badly timed.

For example, you have previously supported the idea of national referenda to circumvent a stagnant political process. But nothing could be more dangerous when a demagogue holds the reins of power. There is nothing a demagogue likes more than to circumvent established forms of lawmaking to project his power and identify his will with the will of the people.

You have also argued for a constitutional convention to propose new amendments. But calling for a constitutional convention just as a demagogue has won the presidency is the worst possible example of political timing. Trump won the 2016 election because he fired up a populist political movement that endorses his call to blow up the system. His followers will surely be major participants in any new constitutional convention. At best the convention would be futile, because the country is now too deeply divided to achieve ratification by three-quarters of the states. At worst it would be dangerous, because Trump's ability to influence both the convention and Republican-controlled state legislatures might result in authoritarian changes to our constitutional system. Even if you are correct that we need new constitutional amendments, the moment for an Article V convention can't arise until the demagogue is thoroughly defeated and discredited.

Conclusion: A Machine That Would Not Go of Itself

There is a famous conceit that the framers sought to create a republican machine that would go of itself, a Newtonian contraption that would check and balance powers so effectively that the republic's continuation would be assured. All later generations have to do is stick to the framers' design and all will be well.

This was always a pipe dream. The framers did not think themselves so omniscient. They knew the history of republics, their frailty and fragility; and they knew their own shortcomings as fallible human beings. Above all, they understood that in the long run no republic can survive without political faith, without the dedication of each generation of its citizens to the public good, and without the continual maintenance of institutions of civil society—including media and educational systems—that support and nourish self-governance.

Over two centuries later, we likewise understand that the machine will not go of itself. It has taken—and will take—the efforts of many people to oppose recurring threats to our democracy and to restore trust in our institutions when our political faith is challenged. What constitutional structure can do is make these tasks easier or harder to achieve. That is why the study of constitutional structure, and what you have called the Constitution of Settlement, is so important.

The American Constitution failed once before, in 1860. It might fail again. But over the years, from the founding to the present, Americans have built their Constitution with the possibility of failure in mind. They have sought to accommodate and incorporate change while limiting the number of constitutional failures—or at the very least minimizing the effects of constitutional failure so that Americans can rebound from it. The framers knew that no constitution is perfect, and that no republic lasts forever. Whether our Constitution works well or badly can only be tested through time and experience. We have come upon such a test right now.

Your devoted friend,
Jack

PART THREE

CONSTITUTIONAL

CRISIS

FEBRUARY 21, 2017

Dear Jack,

What better time than President's Day, a month and a day after Donald Trump's inauguration and a month after roughly one percent of the entire population of the U.S. took to the streets to protest that event, to resume our epistolary exchanges? If one were a visitor from Mars who had no feelings about what is happening to the United States, a posture of fascinated detachment would be completely understandable. If, however, one is a member of the American political community who cares deeply about our collective future, then detachment is scarcely suitable. I find altogether appropriate the lines from Bertolt Brecht's poem "To Those Who Follow in Our Wake": "He who laughs / Has not yet received / The terrible news." Whether or not Donald Trump is accurately described as a sociopath, a lay diagnosis I have tended to offer, there can be little doubt that he is, as agreed upon by an increasing number of pundits across the political spectrum, totally unfit to be president of the United States. [Indeed, by March 2018, that would be almost conventional wisdom, with heartbroken former Republicans like Jennifer Rubin, George Will, or Max Boot often being most caustic in their assessments.] But, of course, he does occupy the White House (when he is not at Mar-a-Lago). And we have to assess the implications of that truly terrible fact.

That the United States is "polarized" has become an almost banal truth about our contemporary polity. The polarization is reminiscent of that often found prior to the breakout of civil war. That is, Americans increasingly ascribe basically "enemy" status to those fellow

Americans who disagree with them. I borrow the use of this term in this context from Carl Schmitt's *The Concept of the Political*, which reinforces my belief that Schmitt is, alas, one of the most important legal and political theorists of the past century. It is no compliment to us that that is the case, but he did accurately discern the role that hatred of putative enemies could play in politics and the tendency to grant executives the power to do whatever they think necessary to confront ostensible "emergencies" warranting extreme measures, whether or not justified by what might be called "normal" constitutionalism.

It is also worth consulting his attack on Weimar parliamentarianism in *The Crisis of Parliamentary Democracy*. For years, I have seen our own Congress accurately described in Schmitt's contempt for the notion that the Weimar Parliament was a truly deliberative body capable of resolving the challenges facing it. Who can have any conceivable respect for Mitch McConnell and Paul Ryan, who every single day prove the irrelevance of Madison's theory in *Federalist* No. 51 that service in the legislature will assure a willingness to check a reckless and dangerous president?

So, far more than you, I remain in at least a semi-apocalyptic frame of mind, frightened both of a dangerously unfit and psychologically unhinged president and of a Congress that seems committed to collaboration so long as they believe he will sign their bills that will, to the maximum feasible extent, undo not only Obamacare and Dodd-Frank, but also much of the Great Society and even the New Deal. Most Americans already "disapprove" of Trump—they have long manifested their contempt of Congress when asked by pollsters—and believe that the country is headed in the wrong direction, as I clearly do. But it is absolutely unclear what the actual relevance of such public opinion is, however widely shared it may be.

Could civil violence—whether or not full-scale civil war—break out? Surely the answer is yes, most likely attached to the viciously cruel policies of deportation of undocumented aliens that appear to be an obsession of the Trump administration. Enforcement of the equally cruel and vicious Fugitive Slave Law, particularly in Boston, helped to trigger the Civil War that engulfed America in 1861. I fully expect many Americans to unite in solidarity with potential deportees (as well as, for that matter, other aliens caught up in the Kafkaesque immigration machinery being devised by the Trump administration). It takes little imagination to imagine an ICE officer, who may in fact feel legitimately threatened by a hostile crowd, using firearms against his (and I use the gendered pronoun advisedly) adversaries; it takes almost as little imagination to imagine that an armed protester will initiate hostilities, perhaps legitimately fearing that the ICE agents are about to open fire themselves. It takes only a bit more imagination to imagine the use by the administration of an agent provocateur to initiate the violence that would lead to a national crackdown in the name of "law and order." [To be sure, that did not happen in the year following this letter. But I think it is foolhardy to assume that the scenario has therefore become irrelevant. The Trump administration in March 2018 is declaring what might be called "legal war" on California for the state's refusal to collaborate with ICE, and one can only wonder what might happen if the administration carries out various threats both to increase levels of deportation and even treat as criminals those public officials who join in protesting this national policy.]

One might recall in this context the decision of the Obama administration, wisely or not, to turn tail and run when federal lands were occupied by Cliven Bundy's livestock. The administration came to the prudent decision that Bundy's armed supporters might well use their arms against federal authorities attempting to seize the livestock that were illegally grazing. I would be astonished if the Trump administration would come to a similar decision in the case of protesters — even if led by nuns and priests — objecting to the roundup of undocumented aliens. The point is that the Trump administration will not have to search far and wide to find precedents — including prosecution of journalists who publish prohibited "leaks" — that will undergird a move toward a far more authoritarian state.

As you know, I also take seriously the possibility that what have heretofore been politically unimportant secessionist movements throughout the United States could in fact become quite significant. The most obvious possibility is California, where vigorous attempts are taking place to collect the roughly 550,000 signatures that would place the state's secession on a 2019 ballot. Our mutual colleague and friend Akhil Amar believes, I suspect like most Americans, that secession is simply "unconstitutional." Period. If one had any doubts about the rightness of Lincoln's basic argument in his First Inaugural, they should have been stilled by the surrender of Lee to Grant at

Appomattox. I confess that I find the constitutional arguments more complicated. I am reluctant to concede that profound issues involving the meaning of government by "consent of the governed" can be settled by force of arms, whatever the prudential wisdom attached to recognizing the truth of Chairman Mao's dictum that political power (usually) grows out of the barrel of a gun.

But I want to conclude this particular missive by raising two points about our formal structures of governance, about which I know you have well-thought-out views that may differ from my own. The first involves the lack in our political system of a formal method of displacing a president through a vote of "no confidence" by, say, two-thirds of Congress assembled together. It is crystal clear that impeachment does not work to get rid of an incompetent and even dangerous president, not least because lawyers start shouting at one another as to whether incompetence and danger constitute the "high Crimes and Misdemeanors" that are a predicate condition for impeachment. The Twenty-Fifth Amendment is manifesting itself, not surprisingly, as a mere "parchment barrier" that Madison would have well understood, since it requires that members of the president's own inner sanctum take the lead in declaring him unable to carry out the solemn duties of the office. One might imagine its utility should a president be clearly and unequivocally physically debilitated, as happened in the assassinations of Garfield and McKinley or in the aftermath of the stroke suffered by Woodrow Wilson in 1919. Mental and emotional debility are entirely different matters, though. We await opening of the relevant papers to know how many White House insiders believed that Ronald Reagan's Alzheimer's disease was already manifesting itself during his second term. We certainly know that no one acted on that belief. At the very least, incidentally, we might support the passage of a law by Congress requiring all presidents to undergo yearly physical and neurological tests, with the results being made public. Why we treat this as protected by some notion of presidential "privacy" is beyond me.

But the Trump administration is also demonstrating in spades the reality of the "alternative government" (with its own "alternative facts") that presidents are now privileged to form. That is, presidents now appoint their own lawyers, national security advisors, economic counselors, and policy "czars" without the slightest accountability to

Congress, either through a confirmation process or, perhaps more importantly, the possibility of compelled testimony through issuance of subpoenas. Both of us have written, separately and together, of the development of the "national security state" following World War II. The best overall study of this reality is by Stephen Griffin, who notes that much has happened not only without adequate public discussion, but also without building up a solid edifice of constitutional "doctrine" that might allow us to know its metes and bounds. The Supreme Court, of course, has been almost no help whatsoever, either writing occasional cryptic decisions or, at least as likely, refusing to engage with the issues by adopting in full the "passive" (or "cowardly") virtues associated with Alexander Bickel. Thus, for example, dubious use of "standing" doctrine or of the "state secrets privilege" has effectively insulated many executive acts from any scrutiny at all.

Those who hate and despise Donald Trump—and see him as a potential harbinger of constitutional dictatorship—must admit that he and his apologists will be able to build on actions and arguments of the Clinton and Obama administrations as well as the Reagan and Bush presidencies. Secure in the belief that "it can't happen here," political liberals have, overall, been as eager to support an enhanced reading of executive power as conservatives, even if they/we often disagree on specific examples. We *have* created what is close to a de facto constitutional dictatorship with regard to the latitude that presidents seem to possess in areas touching especially on military and foreign policy. Is there any genuine possibility of turning back, or must we continue to rely on the American people to have the wisdom to elect tolerable presidents/dictators? But who, after 2016, can have such confidence, especially in a country that continues to rely on the Electoral College to make the choice?

It's an unfortunate truth that we will have many occasions to continue this exchange. There is no reason to believe that the Trump administration will do anything to assuage our plausible worries, even if, at least so far (after one month), we don't seem on the verge of thermonuclear war.

So, even as I join in laughing at Alec Baldwin and John Oliver in their skewerings of our possibly demented president, one must not fall into the trap of settling for a merely decadent posture of laughter or irony. As Brecht suggests, these really are terrible times, and rueful laughter or outright anger must be succeeded by political organization, opposition, and, if it comes to it, resistance.

I hope you can persuade me that I am excessive in my fears and wrong in my analysis.

Sandy

APRIL 14, 2017

Dear Sandy,

As we approach the end of the first 100 days of the Trump presidency, none of the fears that you offered in February appear close to being realized anytime soon. There has been no civil war, no riots in the streets. Out-of-the-mainstream secessionist movements remain just that—out of the mainstream.

We Are Not in a Constitutional Crisis

To be sure, this has not stopped Donald Trump from doing any number of outrageous things. His travel ban—a thinly disguised attempt to implement his campaign promise to keep Muslims out of the United States—is only the most noteworthy. As a result, his critics have begun to speak of a "constitutional crisis" in the United States. I want to take up our exchange once again with this as a starting point. Given our own account of constitutional crises,[1] we can see that we are not currently in a constitutional crisis, but we can also see why the term is so likely to be misused.

A constitutional crisis occurs when there is a serious danger that the Constitution is about to fail at its central task. The central task of constitutions is to keep disagreement within the boundaries of ordinary politics rather than breaking down into anarchy, violence, or civil

---

1. Sanford Levinson and Jack M. Balkin, "Constitutional Crises," *University of Pennsylvania Law Review* 157 (2009): 427.

war. To be sure, constitutions are also valuable because they protect civil liberties and divide and restrain power; but their first job is to keep the peace and make people struggle with each other within politics rather than outside of it.

Constitutional crises come in three types. In the first kind, politicians (or military officials) announce that they won't obey the Constitution. They argue that the Constitution doesn't work or doesn't adequately deal with the current situation so they no longer feel required to follow it. In our system of government, government officials are also supposed to obey judicial orders specifically directed to them. (That is true even if they believe that the judge has interpreted the law incorrectly.) Therefore defying a direct judicial order would also be tantamount to precipitating a constitutional crisis. When government officials (or the military) publicly announce that they will no longer play by the rules of the Constitution, the Constitution has failed. Constitutional crises of this type are very rare in American history.

Second, the Constitution might fail because it keeps political actors from preventing a looming disaster. For example, the Constitution might demand that government officials act—or not act—in a way that leads directly to disaster. Or people may believe that the Constitution makes no provision for a particular event, so that everyone is paralyzed and calamity ensues. In this second type of crisis, everyone goes off the cliff together, like a pack of lemmings. These situations are even rarer than the first type of crisis because political actors (and the courts) usually conclude that the Constitution allows them to innovate and escape disaster.

Third, a constitution might fail because people disagree about what the Constitution means, and they disagree so strongly that they are no longer content to engage in politics and ordinary forms of protest. Instead, people take to the streets and engage in violence. They try to secede from the Union. They attempt a coup or begin a civil war. Widespread rioting breaks out, or the army refuses to obey civilian control. The most important example of this kind of crisis is the American Civil War, when the constitutional system broke down because of intractable disputes over the growth and expansion of slavery.

When people are upset at what government officials have done, they often call these actions constitutional crises. However, most of these situations aren't really constitutional crises, because there is no real danger that the Constitution is about to break down. The vast majority of uses of the term "constitutional crisis" are hyperbole.

Sometimes when people call something a constitutional crisis, they really mean that there is a heated dispute about the best interpretation of the law or the Constitution, and that their political opponents are interpreting the law or the Constitution in the wrong way. That in itself, however, is not a constitutional crisis, because disputes about the best interpretation of the law and of the Constitution are a normal feature of American politics. Many, but not all of these disputes, are eventually settled in the courts. Others are settled through politics. Settlement of serious disputes through the courts or politics is not a constitutional crisis. It is how a constitution is supposed to work.

Sometimes what people call constitutional crises are really what Mark Tushnet has called "constitutional hardball." This is a situation in which political actors stretch or defy political conventions that were previously considered unspoken rules of fair play in politics but were not clearly legally required. People who engage in hardball tactics deliberately violate old norms in order to create new ones and gain a political advantage. This often causes outrage and leads to reprisals in politics. The Republican-controlled Senate's refusal to hold a hearing for anyone President Obama nominated to the Supreme Court in his last year in office was an example of constitutional hardball. The Republican strategy violated what Democrats believed were unspoken norms of political fair play, and it will likely shape how Democrats behave in the future. What happened was not, however, a constitutional crisis. [It might, however, be evidence of what I call "constitutional rot"—a decay in the norms and institutions that sustain a democratic republic. I describe this phenomenon in more detail in my June 18, 2017, letter.]

A more accurate use of the term "constitutional crisis" involves situations in which people reasonably fear that the Constitution will fail in one of the three ways I've just described, even though the breaking point hasn't yet occurred. A constitution that is on the brink of failure is a constitution in crisis.

If President Richard Nixon had refused to obey the Supreme Court's order to surrender the Watergate tapes in 1974, he would have precipitated a constitutional crisis of the first type. People feared that Nixon wouldn't obey, and so one could say that this was a moment of constitutional crisis. Ultimately, however, he did obey the judicial order, and the potential crisis was averted.

Probably the most important constitutional crisis in the nation's history was the secession of the Southern states and the resulting Civil War. This was a crisis of the first type and the third type. Politicians and military officials openly stated that they would refuse to play by the rules of the Constitution: states seceded from the Union and then resisted through violence. That constitutional crisis resulted in enormous bloodshed and suffering, and required the Constitution to be reconstructed with three new amendments.

A constitutional crisis is a very serious thing, because if we were in the middle of a genuine constitutional crisis, there would be a real and serious danger that the Constitution would fail. But, as noted above, most things that people call constitutional crises don't involve serious threats of constitutional failure. In general, one should not confuse heated constitutional disputes with constitutional crises. Similarly, one should not confuse political crises—in which people struggle for power within the limits of the Constitution—with constitutional crises, in which the Constitution itself fails or is on the verge of failing.

When people talk about constitutional crisis in the Trump administration, the first thing that they might have in mind is the flurry of executive orders that began his presidency, and, in particular, his January 27, 2017, executive order on immigration, which is sometimes called a "Muslim ban."

The January 2017 executive order on immigration is very unjust, and there are good arguments that it is unconstitutional.[2] But it has not precipitated a constitutional crisis. The courts often find that the executive branch of the United States government has violated the law or the Constitution, but that doesn't make each of these situations a constitutional crisis.

On the other hand, if President Trump ordered executive branch officials to defy judicial orders, and they did so, not merely in isolated instances out of confusion, but deliberately and consistently,

---

2. The lower federal courts struck down the first two versions of the ban. In the spring of 2018, the U.S. Supreme Court upheld a third version, explaining that it would not assume that the order was motivated by unconstitutional animus toward Muslims if there was a plausible national security justification. *Trump v. Hawaii*, 585 U.S. __ (2018).

that could precipitate a constitutional crisis. If President Trump announced that he would not follow the Constitution, if he arrested members of the Supreme Court, or if he defied a direct judicial order, that would mark a constitutional crisis.

As you and I pointed out in our original piece, American politicians almost never announce that they will go outside the Constitution or the law. Instead, they argue that they are complying with the law based on their interpretation of it.

One might object that this allows politicians to violate the Constitution if they just lie about their motivations or if their legal positions are objectively unreasonable. But there is a reason why forcing politicians to state their positions in terms of legality and constitutionality is important to constitutional government. This means that they are still publicly adhering to a political norm that everyone must obey the law and the Constitution. When politicians obey this norm, it drives controversies back into the courts or into ordinary politics for resolution. Achieving this result is what constitutions are supposed to do. To be sure, when people argue about what the law means or what the Constitution means, it is often very upsetting, because politicians often have incentives to make specious or disingenuous claims to justify their actions. But as long as the courts are open and are obeyed, this by itself does not produce a constitutional crisis.

Crisis is not the same thing as injustice. Many unjust things happen in a constitutional system without precipitating a constitutional crisis. Constitutions make politics possible, and politics is often unjust.

You can tell if you are in a constitutional crisis when politicians stop saying that they will comply with the law, with judicial orders, or with the Constitution. Or you can tell that you are in a constitutional crisis when there is widespread civil unrest or rebellion. Until that happens, you are not in a constitutional crisis, and for that, at least, you can be thankful.

Why Have Our Institutions Held Up So Far?

To be sure, all is not well in these United States of America. The new administration has made many ill-considered policy decisions—some of which will haunt us for many years to come. The inquiry into Russia's tampering with the 2016 election proceeds day by day, and the president himself seems as ignorant and mercurial as ever. There is also the looming question of how he will deal with the mounting threat from North Korea.

Yet, remarkably, for those who saw Trump as the second coming of Mussolini (or worse), it may be worthwhile to step back and consider why Trump the demagogue has remained—so far—only a demagogue and not become a dictator; and why he has been repeatedly stymied in many of his most important initiatives during the first 100 days. The answers, I think, have a lot to do with our previous discussions about the structure of the American constitutional system. The experience of the first 100 days also tends to confirm my central prediction about the Trump presidency. He is not a dictator but a disjunctive president, presiding over the dissolution of the Reagan regime.

Why hasn't Trump been able to work his will more effectively? Because the various institutions of government—both formal and informal—have stopped him.

Begin with civil society. Trump is, and remains, a particularly unpopular president. There have been sustained protests against his administration from its inception. Donations have flowed to groups like the ACLU to help fight his policies. The institutions of mass culture—from late night television shows to YouTube—regularly make fun of him. Mocking Trump has reinforced the idea that he is not someone to be feared. Successful dictators inspire caution and silence. Trump inspires ridicule.

Journalism is an especially important segment of civil society. Media organizations were deeply compromised by the 2016 election, as they accepted the Faustian bargain of increased ratings and sensational coverage in exchange for a Trump presidency. Although many individual journalists did an outstanding job during the 2016 campaign, the media as a whole have no one but themselves to blame for hyping Hillary's e-mails and normalizing The Donald's demagoguery.

Yet Trump's ascendancy to the presidency seems to have stiffened the media's spine and caused media organizations to rethink the vocation of the journalist. Trump has obliged, labeling the media "the opposition" and "the enemy of the American people." There is nothing so likely to energize and inspire American journalists than a president who abuses them in this way. If this were truly a dictatorship, media organizations would cower, be bought off, or be closed down. Instead, the media is energized and warming to its oppositional role.

Trump, to be sure, still has his propaganda arms in the media—Fox News and Breitbart—but the vast majority of the mainstream media does not seem very afraid of him. Although Trump has tried to punish the media by selectively manipulating and withdrawing access, he has not been able to render them docile. And slowly but surely, through trial and error, media organizations are starting to learn his standard tricks of media manipulation.

Next, consider the coordinate branches of government. The judiciary remains independent. To be sure, Trump has not yet been able to appoint many judges.[3] But the one important exception, Justice Neil Gorsuch, ironically shows the limits of his power. Dictators generally try to stock the courts with loyalists and cronies, who can be counted on to sacrifice the rule of law to defend the leader's power. That does not appear to be happening, at least not yet. In order to win over skeptical conservatives during the Republican primaries, Trump pledged to appoint judges from a list put together with help from the Federalist Society and the Heritage Foundation. These groups hew to movement conservative ideology, not to Trumpism. Gorsuch is a Federalist society pick, not a Trump pick. (Indeed, Trump doesn't even appear to *have* a judicial philosophy—other than the slogans he has learned to repeat at rallies to gain applause.)

Because Trump has essentially delegated judicial selection to the conservative legal movement, there is no reason to believe that his judges will be especially loyal to him. Rather, we should expect that they will be loyal to conservative ideology and to conservative visions of the Constitution and laws. To be sure, if litigation raises questions that divide conservatives and liberals, and if the position Trump takes aligns with the conservative position (for example, on issues of federalism or abortion rights), then the judges he appoints will probably support his position. But that is because of their desire to promote conservative constitutional values, and not merely because it would benefit Trump.

One of the ironies of Trump's ascension, in other words, is that it may make the judiciary *more* independent of him, even though the judiciary will remain strongly polarized between liberals and con-

3. Senate Majority Leader Mitch McConnell soon corrected this deficiency, placing a high priority on judicial confirmations. During the first two years of the Trump administration, the Senate confirmed Trump appointees to lower federal courts at a brisk pace.

servatives. This is the opposite of what usually occurs with successful dictatorships. Instead of installing a bevy of Trumpista flunkies, he is likely to appoint a series of Federalist Society favorites. If he wants conservative judges to uphold his policies and positions, he will have to become more predictably conservative or, at the very least, take more predictably conservative positions in litigation. All of this pushes Trump toward behaving like a traditional conservative Republican.

[There is an important caveat to this analysis. Even if Trump's appointees are not especially loyal to him, they might be unconsciously motivated to protect the interests of the Republican Party in their assessments of what the law requires. That might be especially important if the Mueller investigation leads to federal court litigation—for example, on whether the president must respond to a subpoena to testify. The more that the party's fortunes are bound up with Trump's, the more Republican-appointed judges might protect him.]

The early litigation over Trump's immigration orders revealed that federal judges are deeply skeptical of Trump's command of national security issues. Generally speaking, federal judges defer to the executive on national security questions. But in the litigation over the immigration orders, federal judges cut him little slack. They doubted whether his orders actually promoted national security. To be sure, conservative judges (including those that Trump will likely appoint) are considerably more likely to defer to the executive on these issues, but it remains a genuine question how much they will defer to this president.

Generally speaking, judges understand that national security decisions are vetted by experts with special knowledge and long experience in foreign policy. But the Trump White House is full of neophytes and buffoons. There is no particular reason to defer to a carload of clowns on the most dangerous issues that face a republic. That is especially so if judges suspect that Trump and many of his subordinates are prejudiced against Muslims. Until the White House demonstrates its competence, there may be a "Trump discount" in national security that applies to this administration only.[4]

4. In the travel ban case, *Trump v. Hawaii*, 585 U.S. __ (2018), however, the Supreme Court refused to accept a Trump discount. Chief Justice John Roberts explained that the Supreme Court would uphold Trump's travel ban because "we must consider not only the statements of a particular President, but also the authority of the Presidency itself." Justice Anthony Kennedy, who retired shortly the opinion was announced, cast

Next, turn to Congress. Why has Trump been unable—at least as of the time of this letter—to repeal and replace Obamacare? Because of standard features of the constitutional system: (1) bicameralism—that is, the need to please both the House and the Senate; (2) internal rules of the Senate, including the filibuster and the rules on reconciliation; (3) party polarization, which meant that Trump would have to get virtually all of his votes from the Republican caucus; and (4) federalism—the countervailing influence of Republican governors in red states who object to curtailing Obama's Medicaid expansion.

These features made it especially difficult for Trump and the Republicans to repeal Obamacare. Complete repeal was not possible through reconciliation and would require sixty votes in the Senate—a nonstarter because of party polarization. Yet a measure consistent with reconciliation rules—which could be passed by Republican votes alone—would keep much of Obamacare in place. It also had to lower taxes for the wealthy. The result was a dog's lunch of a bill that threw millions off health insurance and undermined Medicaid in the red states that had already adopted the Medicaid expansion. Such a bill could not command unanimity among Republicans.

The unintended consequences of the increasing party polarization that allowed the Republicans to gain majority status will ultimately destroy the regime. This is the cunning of history at work. Conservative movement politics was able to succeed politically by promoting and then exacerbating party polarization. This was Newt Gingrich's signal insight. Increasing party polarization, in turn, leads to parliamentary-style parties in a presidential system. By this, I mean that the two parties eventually become ideologically very far apart, agree on very little substantively, and neither party is willing to cooperate in the other party's central legislative initiatives.

As polarization continues, the strategy of each party is to refuse to cooperate so the other party will be blamed. The goal is to leverage popular discontent to throw the other party out of power in subsequent elections so that one's own party can gain both the White House and control of Congress. As the Obama presidency demonstrated, when the parties are strongly polarized, these are the conditions for getting anything important accomplished in Congress.

---

the deciding vote, explaining that on questions of immigration and foreign policy, it was up to the political branches, and not the courts, to ensure compliance with the Constitution.

This is what I mean when I say that during the Reagan regime, the United States has developed parliamentary-style parties in a presidential system. Obviously, the 1787 Constitution was not designed for parliamentary-style parties. As a result, the constitutional system works badly both in terms of representation and efficiency. And it works badly not only for competent presidents, but also for venal demagogues like Donald Trump.

Ideological polarization has a further, unintended consequence: It makes presidents increasingly hostage to their own party's internal coherence and discipline. A Republican president must count on a unified Republican caucus to succeed. Because Democrats will not cooperate with Republicans (and vice versa), nothing important can be achieved unless Republicans are unified.

And there's the rub: As a political regime proceeds, it becomes increasingly difficult to maintain political unity. The coalition becomes factionalized and certain factions become radical, demanding that they get their own way and refusing compromise.

Ironically, the Republican Party's success at gerrymandering House districts (to maintain majority control) has enhanced these tendencies toward factionalism and radicalization. Many Freedom Caucus members, for example, are in safe districts produced by successful Republican Party gerrymanders. They don't compromise with congressional leadership because they don't have to.

As a result, by the middle of the Obama administration, congressional Republicans, who were united in their opposition to Obama (and Obamacare), nevertheless found themselves in the middle of a civil war. Their inability to work together led to the resignation of John Boehner as Speaker of the House and the ascension of Paul Ryan, who believed (or at least hoped) that he would bring the warring factions together. Trump's campaign for the presidency papered over these disputes for a while, but they reemerged with a vengeance as soon as the Trump administration attempted to push a bill through Congress.

Today, we see the fruits of the Reagan regime in its final days: a polarized Congress with a Republican majority that must rely on party discipline to succeed but can only rarely achieve it (except, of course, where lower taxes for the donor class are concerned). It is likely that no Republican president—whether Mitt Romney, Marco Rubio, or Ted Cruz—could govern effectively under these circumstances. Under the leadership of Donald Trump, a petulant narcissist with no understanding of policy, successful bridging of differences is even less likely.

Even the success of the Gorsuch nomination is a sign of a regime on its last legs. As a regime proceeds, the judiciary becomes an increasingly important partner in promoting the regime's commitments of ideology and interest. A party that knows that it will not be dominant forever rationally seeks to entrench its allies in life-tenured positions in the judiciary. It does this not only to promote its constitutional values but also to defend against future control by the political opposition. That is one reason why Republicans, perhaps even more than Democrats, regard judicial appointments—and control of the federal judiciary—as incredibly important.

In the early years of a regime, the goal of politicians is to keep holdover judges from the old regime from blocking change and to replace these holdovers with judges friendly to the new regime. Late in the regime, by contrast, the strategy changes. The dominant party's control over the national political process is far more tenuous. Therefore, the goal is to get as much accomplished as possible through doctrinal development and to defend against an increasingly uncertain future. Late in the regime, lawyers ideologically allied with the regime jettison earlier calls for judicial restraint. Increasingly, they want robust judicial review that pushes the boundaries of existing doctrine to further the regime's ideology and constitutional values.

Put another way, early in the Reagan regime, Republicans wanted judges to stop interfering with police officers and second-guessing school boards; late in the regime, they want judges to strike down the Voting Rights Act, kneecap public-sector unions, and protect corporate speech. As the Reagan regime slowly grinds to its conclusion, and the political branches are mired in gridlock, the federal judiciary becomes an increasingly important site for effective conservative policymaking, and an increasingly valuable prize of conservative politics. After all, if Republicans can't get anything done in Congress, there is always the Supreme Court.

Desperate times call for desperate measures. That is why the Republicans were willing to play constitutional hardball—not once, but twice—with the Supreme Court nomination process. They refused to hold any hearings on Merrick Garland, and they eliminated the filibuster on Supreme Court nominations to install Neil Gorsuch. Republicans understood that if Obama could replace Scalia with Garland, they might lose control of the highest court in the federal judiciary for many years. All of the conservative litigation campaigns currently in motion would be for naught. They needed to preserve a Republican majority on the Supreme Court at all costs. In fact, the more inept that the political branches prove themselves to be, the more important it is that the one institution that can effectively make and enforce policy — the United States Supreme Court — stays in the hands of the Republican Party and the conservative movement.

The first 100 days of the Trump administration suggest that Trump is in the same structural position as Herbert Hoover and Jimmy Carter — an unorthodox candidate trying to hold together the fraying coalition of an exhausted regime. Moreover, I also believe that much of what hinders Trump are features of the Constitution of Settlement that prevent majorities from working their will too easily.

In sum, both the Constitution of Settlement *and* the exhaustion of the Reagan regime are limiting Trump's ability to be a successful demagogue, much less a dictator. Our constitutional system may be unwieldy, but it reveals distinctive advantages when threatened by a demagogue.

All this, of course, is merely evidence for my thesis, not a decisive confirmation. The vagaries of politics instruct — and humble — all of us; and it has not yet been 100 days.

Jack

PART FOUR

CONSTITUTIONAL ROT

JUNE 18, 2017

Dear Sandy,

People continue to be obsessed with Donald Trump's remarkable rise to power and his even more remarkable presidency. It's hard to avoid thinking about the scandals swirling around him day to day. While these are important, they are not the subject of this letter. Instead, as we have done before in this exchange, I want to look at the big picture. In this picture, Trump is merely a symptom. He is a symptom of a serious problem with our political and constitutional system.

Trump outrages and flusters his opponents; so much so, that as we lurch from controversy to controversy, many people wonder whether we are currently in some sort of constitutional crisis. As I explained in my last letter, we are not. Rather, we are in a period of constitutional rot.

By "constitutional rot," I mean a decay in the features of our system that maintain it as a healthy democracy and a healthy republic. Constitutional rot has been going on for some time in the United States, and it has produced our current dysfunctional politics.

Constitutional dysfunction isn't the same thing as gridlock—after all, the three branches of government are currently controlled by the same party. Rather, it is a problem of *representation*. Over time, our political system has become less democratic and less republican. It has become increasingly oligarchical.

By "democratic," I mean responsive to popular will and popular opinion. By "republican," I mean that representatives are devoted to the public good and responsive to the interests of the public as a whole—as opposed to a small group of powerful individuals and groups. When representatives are responsive not to the interests of the public in general but to a relatively small group of individuals and groups, we have oligarchy.

Republics Are Especially Susceptible to Constitutional Rot

Republics are governments premised on the pursuit of the common good. Representatives are given power for the sole purpose of achieving the public good. The framers of our Constitution understood that republics are fragile things. They are easily corrupted, and over time they are likely to turn into oligarchies or autocracies.

When a government becomes oligarchical, leaders spend less and less time working for the public good. Instead, they spend more and more time enriching a small group of important backers that keep them in power. Because the general public feels abandoned by politicians, it gradually loses faith in the political system. This leads to the rise of demagogues, who flatter people with promises that they will make everything right again.

In the United States, oligarchy has resulted from the gradual breakdown of the party system that selects candidates and keeps political parties responsive to the public. It has also resulted from changes in how political campaigns are financed and from long-term changes in the structure of mass media, which have encouraged political distrust, exacerbated polarization, and merged politics with entertainment.

Both parties have been affected by these developments, but the problems are especially pronounced in the Republican Party, which styles itself as a populist party but is anything but. A small class of wealthy donors has disproportionate control over the Republican policy agenda. The influence of the donor class over that agenda is the best explanation of developments in Congress.

What are the deeper causes of constitutional rot? There are four interlocking features, which we might call the Four Horsemen of constitutional rot: (1) political polarization; (2) loss of trust in government; (3) increasing economic inequality; and (4) policy disasters, a term coined by Stephen Griffin to describe important failures in decision making by our representatives, like the Vietnam War, the Iraq War, and the 2008 financial crisis.

Today one of the most important, overarching policy failures is America's inadequate response to globalization. The 2008 financial crisis is a special case of this larger policy failure.

A democracy requires a broad-based, stable, and economically secure middle class to create the right incentives for government officials to pursue the public good. If economic inequality gets too pronounced, the wealthiest tend to grab disproportionate political power, and they will use it to further entrench and enrich themselves. A globalized economy threatens a broad-based, stable, and economically secure middle class because it puts serious pressure on social insurance programs and on the economic stability and self-sufficiency of Americans.

Political and economic elites have not navigated globalization's changes well. They have taken pretty good care of themselves, but they have not taken care of the whole country. This inadequate response to globalization has hastened constitutional rot.

These Four Horsemen—polarization, loss of trust, economic inequality, and policy disaster—mutually reinforce each other. Political scientists have pointed out that rising economic inequality exacerbates polarization, which in turn helps produce policies that exacerbate inequality. Rising inequality and polarization also encourage loss of trust. Polarization and oligarchy create overconfidence and insulate decision makers from necessary criticism, which makes policy disasters more likely; policy disasters, in turn, further undermine trust in government, and so on.

In an oligarchical system, regardless of its formal legal characteristics, a relatively small number of backers effectively decide who stays in power. In such a system, politicians will have strong incentives to divert resources to the relatively small group of backers who keep them in power. Not surprisingly, the power of government and resources for government are often wasted or diverted from important public goods. Our constitutional system is still formally democratic, but it has become more oligarchical in practice over time. As a result, the United States has wasted a great deal of money on policy disasters, it has shaped the tax code so that most of the benefits of economic growth have gone to the wealthiest Americans, and through unwise tax and fiscal policy, it has diverted a lot of money that could have been used for public services and public goods to the wealthy.

Constitutional Defenses against Constitutional Rot

Our Constitution is designed to ward off both oligarchy and demagogues and to preserve a republic. For the most part, it has been quite
successful in the face of a wide variety of changes and challenges.
Some of these features of our constitutional system, however, don't
work very well anymore in preventing oligarchical tendencies. Separation of powers between Congress and the president is a good example.
Rick Pildes and Daryl Levinson have pointed out that our system is
better described as a separation of parties rather than a separation of
powers. When the president and Congress are from the same party,
there will be little oversight of the president. The Republican Congress's almost complete disinterest in checking Donald Trump is a particularly worrisome example.

Even so, the United States still has many other republican defenses.
We still have an independent judiciary, regular elections, and a free
press. Many other countries that have eventually succumbed to autocracy are not so fortunate. Moreover, in the United States, from the
founding onward, lawyers have played a crucial role in defending the
republic: in staffing an independent judiciary, in promoting rule-of-
law values in the bureaucracy, and in bringing cases to protect constitutional rights and check executive overreach. Once again, many
other countries that have become autocratic are not as fortunate as
the United States.

Propaganda and Constitutional Rot

One should not underestimate the value of our free press, even as it
comes under assault from the Trump administration. Reporters have
not been cowed into silence as they have been in other countries. If
anything, Trump's shenanigans and his successful manipulation of the
press in 2016 have caused the press to think more deeply about its
democratic responsibilities.

Even so, the power of the press to protect republican government
has been weakened. Part of this is due to economics, and part of it is
due to other factors. The American system of freedom of the press was
seriously undermined in 2016. It was undermined not by state censor-
ship but by Trump's very effective hacking of the media; he has proved

to be both a master manipulator and a very effective demagogue in the digital era.

The system of free press was also undermined by the production of effective propaganda, both from within the United States and from outside it. These two forms of propaganda come from different sources, but they reinforced each other in a perfect storm in 2016.

We now have domestic propaganda machines that have thrown their support behind Trump and now engage in shameless forms of propaganda that would have done Soviet-era apparatchiks proud. The only difference is that instead of propping up communism, they prop up Trump. In addition, Russia and allied groups in Eastern Europe engaged in successful propaganda campaigns during the 2016 election season, designed to enhance Trump's chances and sow discord and confusion in the United States.

Propaganda's effects corrode republican institutions and encourage constitutional rot. Propaganda enhances polarization; it increases distrust of political opponents, as well as those elements of government held by one's political opponents.

Propaganda tries to foster controversies that divide the country and enhance mutual distrust and hatred among fellow citizens. It seeks to convert politics into a particularly brutal opposition between virtuous friends and evil enemies who must be stopped at all costs and by any means necessary.

Propaganda also undermines the crucial role of deliberation and the search for truth in a democracy. Propaganda attempts to put everything in dispute, so that nothing can be established as true, and everything becomes a matter of personal opinion or partisan belief. Because everything is a matter of opinion, one can assume that anything a political opponent says can be disregarded, and that factual claims contrary to one's own beliefs can also be disregarded. Thus, successful propaganda builds on motivated reasoning and encourages even more motivated reasoning. It undermines shared criteria of reasoning, good-faith attempts at deliberation, and mutual accommodation between political opponents in democracies.

Moreover, if people stop believing in the truth of what they read, they don't have to think hard about political questions. Instead, they can simply make political decisions based on identity or affiliation with their political allies. Propaganda, in other words, undermines

truth to destroy the concept of the public good and to encourage trib-
alism.

As a political system becomes increasingly oligarchical, it also becomes less equal and more polarized, and it generates greater distrust,
both of government in general and of political opponents. People not
only lose trust in government, but in other people who disagree with
them. Political opponents appear less as fellow citizens devoted to the
common good and more like internal threats to the nation.

Another way of putting it is that in a well-functioning republic,
there are friends and potential friends. Potential friends are people
you currently disagree with, but might ally with in the future because
both of you are devoted to the public good. In system of constitutional
rot, the country falls into something like Carl Schmitt's view that all
politics is divided between friends and enemies. From the perspective
of a well-functioning republic, Schmitt's friend/enemy distinction is a
corruption of politics, rather than its essential nature.

Trump as a Symptom of Constitutional Rot

Loss of trust in the government and in political opponents eventually
produces demagogues who attempt to take advantage of the situation.
Demagogues don't spring up unawares. People see them coming from
miles away. But by this point, people have so lost faith in government
that they are willing to gamble on a demagogue. They hope that the
demagogue can make things right again and restore past glories.

Trump is a demagogue. We might even say that he is straight out
of central casting for demagogues: unruly, uncouth, mendacious, dishonest, and cunning. His rise is a symptom of constitutional rot and
constitutional dysfunction. Constitutional rot not only allowed Trump
to rise to power; he also has incentives to increase and exacerbate constitutional rot to stay in power. Many of his actions as president—and
his media strategy—make sense from this perspective.

Polarization helps keep Trump in power, because it binds his supporters to him. He exacerbates polarization by fomenting outrage and
internal division. He also confuses and distracts people, keeping them
off balance and in a state of emotional upheaval. Emotional upheaval,
in turn, increases fear, and fear increases mutual distrust.

Trump doesn't care if his opponents hate him, as long as his base
hates and fears his political opponents more. Because his supporters

hate and fear his enemies, they are more likely to cling to him, because they are quite certain that his enemies are even worse.

Polarization also helps keeps most professional politicians in his party from abandoning him. Many Republican politicians do not trust Trump, and many regard him as unqualified. But if Republican politicians turn on Trump, they will be unable to achieve anything during one of the infrequent periods in which they control both Congress and the White House. This will infuriate their base and anger the wealthy group of donors who help keep Republicans in power. Republican politicians who oppose Trump may face primary challenges. Finally, Republican politicians can't be sure that enough of their fellow politicians will follow them if they stick their necks out. In fact, they may provoke a civil war within the Republican Party, in which Trump's supporters accuse them of stabbing Trump (and the party) in the back.

Many people think that the sense of upheaval that Trump has created in American politics means that he cannot keep going this way for long; and that his presidency is about to crack apart at any moment. This is a mistake. Polarization and upheaval are good for him. Crisis is his brand.

Why Trump Has Been a Populist Turncoat

If you understand the relationship between polarization and oligarchy, you will understand a remarkable feature of American politics. Although Trump ran as a populist who promised to protect the working class from the depredations of globalization, as soon as he entered the White House, he reversed course. His cabinet is full of wealthy individuals, and many of his top advisors are from the very financial class that he excoriated in his campaign. Moreover, he has quickly allied himself with the most conservative elements of the Republican Party, and he has supported a health care bill that is likely to harm many working-class Americans.

The Republican Party in Congress depends on its donor class to stay in power. The central goal of the Republican agenda, therefore, is to deliver benefits to the donor class, either through tax cuts, government expenditures, or deregulation.

The current health care bill passed in the House and awaiting action in the Senate is a case in point. It is actually a tax cut disguised as a health care measure. It offers a $600 billion tax cut to the wealthiest

Americans, which it pays for by removing some of Obamacare's insurance protections and gradually eliminating its Medicaid expansion. The health care bill's tax cut also sets the revenue baseline that will be used to evaluate tax reform in the next fiscal year, when the Republicans will once again use the reconciliation procedure to pass a bill that cannot be filibustered in the Senate. By locking in tax cuts in the health care bill, Republicans hope to make tax reforms easier to accomplish in ways that are more likely to please their donors.

From the standpoint of populism, the health care bill is an utter travesty; it withdraws important benefits and protections from working-class Americans to benefit the very wealthiest. But it makes perfect sense from the standpoint of oligarchy. Even so-called moderate Republicans in the Senate depend heavily on the donor class, and therefore they face enormous pressures to cave and support the bill by adopting a face-saving (but ineffectual) compromise. Something similar happened in the House. Establishment and more moderate Republicans also caved, not because the Freedom Caucus is so powerful, but because the powerful donors who shape the party's policy agenda wanted their tax cuts. Moreover, because the Senate bill is likely to be so unpopular among the general public, Senate Republicans are drafting it in secret, with no public hearings. The actual text won't be revealed until shortly before the vote is taken. After all, as one Senate aide explained, the Republicans aren't stupid. They know that the bill is toxic. But it pleases their donors, and so they will sacrifice any pretense of procedural regularity to achieve their goals.

The health care bill is a prime example of constitutional rot. Our nominally republican system of government has become so infected by oligarchy that the party in power has no scruples about acting in an entirely shameless manner, as long as the interests of its masters are well-served.

[Although disagreements among Republicans ultimately prevented them from repealing Obamacare, they eventually dismantled one of its key provisions, the individual mandate to purchase insurance, as part of their tax bill passed in December 2017. The repeal allowed them to fund further tax cuts for the wealthy, as discussed in my November 6th letter, below. The tax bill was also rushed through with a minimum of public vetting. Congressional Republicans repeatedly misled the public about what the bill would do, largely because its central goal was to lower taxes on corporations and on the wealthiest Americans.]

Which brings us back to Trump's about-face. Trump ran as a populist, but he now governs as a sellout. This is not an unusual phenomenon among populist revolutionaries. Once they take power, they often quickly discard the people who put them in power; they substitute new backers who are easier to deal with and/or pay off to stay in power.

Trump is a huckster, with few actual ideological commitments. So he has few qualms about changing course. It is much easier for Trump to ally himself with congressional Republicans than to attempt a seriously populist legislative agenda, which would be very costly and would be opposed by members of his own party. Working across the aisle with Democrats is unlikely because of the very polarization Trump has helped foster. Democrats do not trust him, and working with them might lead his Republican allies in Congress to abandon him. And he needs loyalty among Republicans to fend off the scandals swirling around him.

Thus, ironically, Trump's very strategies for gaining power—dividing the country and fomenting mutual hatred—mean that he should align his policies with members of his own party against the Democrats. That means that he will not govern as an economic populist, although his rhetoric will remain rabidly populist. But there will be little substance behind it. It is far easier to align with congressional Republicans, who will protect him from Democrats, who despise him and want to topple him with scandals.

Having cast his lot with congressional Republicans, that means that he, too, will serve the same donor class. Trump may have run a populist campaign, but now that he is in power, he has pretty much embraced oligarchy. His populism is mostly sloganeering—it is a Potemkin village. We might say that it takes a Potemkin village to make a Trump presidency.

The Future

That's the bad news. Here is the good news.

First, as I've argued in my previous letters, Trump represents the end of a cycle of politics rather than the future of politics. The Reagan regime's electoral coalition is falling apart; from 1992 to 2016, the Republican Party won the presidential popular vote only once; twice the party has had to depend on an Electoral College victory. This is a sign of weakness, not strength. In the next few election cycles, a new regime will begin, offering the possibility of a new beginning in American politics.

Second, despite the influx of propaganda and the decline of separation of powers in restraining the president, many features of the constitutional system remain robust. We still have an independent judiciary, a free press, and regular elections.

Third, as we've discussed before, one should not confuse what's been happening in the past several months with constitutional crisis. Constitutional crisis means that the Constitution is no longer able to keep disagreement within politics; as a result, people go outside the law and/or turn to violence or insurrection. However unpleasant our politics may be, all of our current struggles are still within politics.

Fourth, we are headed for a big showdown in electoral politics over the next several election cycles. One of the two parties will have to find a way to restore trust in government and renounce oligarchical politics. The next decade will tell the tale. I remain hopeful.

Even if Trump left office tomorrow, and was replaced with Mike Pence, there would still have to be a reckoning over these issues. Indeed, even if Hillary Clinton had won the election, there would still have to be a reckoning—perhaps even more urgently if Clinton won, because she ran a campaign that paid so little attention to populist concerns. The United States has failed to reconcile globalization with democracy. It has not accommodated the demands of republican government to global economic change. This is a serious policy failure, and it has contributed to constitutional rot. The bill for this neglect is coming due. We will have to pay it.

The central question of constitutional and political reform is how to preserve republican government in the face of a changing global economy. This is not the first time that the American experiment in democracy has been threatened by oligarchy, although the problem arises each time in a different form. The Jacksonians fought the financial aristocracy of their day, the early Republican Party fought the Slave Power, and the populists and progressives fought the "malefactors of great wealth" who dominated the country during its First Gilded Age. Now, in our Second Gilded Age, there is no guarantee that the pattern of success will continue. Even so, Americans should organize themselves on the assumption that they have the ability to defend republican government from oligarchy as they have done many times before.

I believe we will get through this, together. But we have to pay attention to the real sources of constitutional dysfunction, halt the rot that threatens our constitutional system, and preserve our republic. The history of the American Constitution is a series of struggles for greater democracy, equality, and inclusiveness in the face of well-entrenched opposition. Trump's presidency signals the beginning of yet another contest.

Jack

JUNE 24, 2017

Dear Jack,

Let me address your valuable notion of constitutional rot. I'm not sure I agree, even though you base your argument on our own coauthored examination of the concept of constitutional crisis, that "rot" itself isn't an indication of a genuine crisis of the constitutional order. As you argue, any constitutional order that is presumably predicated on the precept, found in the Declaration of Independence, that government should be based on "the consent of the governed" must necessarily start foundering if more and more of the populace at large becomes alienated from government and refuses to see in it anything that can plausibly be regarded as reflecting the necessary quanta of consent. You noted, in our article, that the notion of crisis is especially illuminating in a medical context, when one is unsure that a patient will live or die. Will the fever break, in which case all is well, or will it prove resistant to all antibiotics with dire consequences? So is the "rot" that you spell out a genuine fever that is attacking the organs of our entire system? When a majority of Americans (with which I would associate myself) consistently believe that the country is going in the wrong direction and disapprove, quite strongly, of both the Congress and the executive—and, for that matter, disapprove, albeit less strongly, even of the Supreme Court—can we possibly view ours as a healthy polity? You express genuine optimism, especially toward the end of your most recent missive, in the resilience of our institutions, that this (i.e., the malevolent sociopathy and the sheer ignorance of the Trump presidency and its enablers in Congress), too, shall pass. I certainly don't think this is impossible, but I am, not for the first time, less optimistic (or complacent?) than you are.

I begin by focusing on your comment that "our constitutional system is still formally democratic." As the author of *Our Undemocratic Constitution*, I beg to differ. And as Michael Klarman has magnificently demonstrated, the Constitution's framers were distinctly suspicious of "democracy" and wrote those suspicions into our basic institutional framework. Morton Horwitz once wrote that "democracy" did not become a truly positive term in American constitutional discourse, at least within the Supreme Court, until the twentieth century. In any event, when the framers wrote of a "Republican Form of Government," they were not thinking of a government overly sensitive to the views and preferences of most of the people actually living within the country in 1787. Most, of course, could not participate in government at all: think only of women and slaves, even if one concedes that some states allowed free blacks to vote. But many states at the time had property qualifications for the suffrage, not to mention that the quite large territories encompassed by congressional districts were correctly thought to give significant advantages to elites running for office against the great unwashed.

Our system is "formally democratic" if one focuses on the frequency of elections—we conduct more elections more frequently than any other country in the world—and the undoubted fact that access to the ballot has become considerably more inclusive since the bad old days of the late eighteenth century. That is all to the good. But we should recognize more than I'm afraid we do that such unmodified institutions as bicameralism, the Electoral College, the equal state vote in the Senate, and the presidential veto call into question the extent to which we should so complacently describe ourselves as living even in a formally democratic system. Although not constitutionally required, our fixation on single-member districts (thanks to an 1842 congressional statute), coupled with the near-universal practice in the United States of "first past the post" elections, further limits what could have become a more genuinely "democratic" political system.

I have earlier set out the reasons for my disappointment and even anger at Bernie Sanders for wasting the opportunity of a lifetime to teach his followers—most of whom, I suspect, know almost nothing about the mechanics of the American political system—that the system was rigged in 1787 and needs significant reform if a truly progressive politics is ever to become possible. It is no coincidence that the great changes that the left celebrates all occurred under truly extraordinary—even "emergency"—conditions where the ordinary checks and balances of our byzantine system were somewhat relaxed. That is, the Reconstruction Amendments relied on both the death of 750,000 Americans (including would-be secessionists) and the exclusion of Southern representation from the 1866 Congress that proposed the Fourteenth Amendment (not to mention the military takeover of the Southern governments to procure the ratification of the amendment that would otherwise have never occurred). The New Deal relied on what Arthur Schlesinger Jr. termed "the crisis of the old order" and the brute fact that many Americans, including pundits like Walter Lippmann, entreated FDR simply to declare himself a de facto dictator and engage in rule by decree. He didn't have to do so, thanks to overwhelming Democratic majorities in Congress, who were often willing to pass bills that they had barely read or debated. But, as Ira Katznelson has so well demonstrated, even then southerners retained enough power to assure that African Americans would scarcely benefit from the most important measures of the New Deal.

The third great period of fundamental reform took full advantage of the assassination of John F. Kennedy, who with regard to domestic issues could be described as a relatively tepid president, and the decision of the Republican Party to nominate Barry Goldwater in 1964, which provided the basis for a genuine landslide (and legitimation) of Lyndon Johnson's grandiose (and admirable) desire to outdo FDR in the fields of civil rights and fighting a war on poverty. All of that basically collapsed with the Vietnam War's taking center stage by 1966 and then, more certainly, with the election of Richard Nixon in 1968 (even if we can wax nostalgic about Nixon being the last New Deal president). We must then jump forward to the halcyon days of the first half of Barack Obama's first term, when he was able to push through an (inadequate) stimulus program, a (flawed) reform of the American health care delivery system, and some modest but important reforms of the American banking system. But the Obama administration was basically neutralized after 2011.

And both of us agree that Hillary Clinton's election, however welcome in contrast to Donald Trump's, would have done almost nothing to allow serious confrontation with our most pressing domestic problems. Had she been elected, the tone of our exchanges would have been almost as depressing to read, for we would be emphasizing continuing gridlock and the total opposition of a Republican-controlled House, not to mention the possibility that the House would also be trying to impeach her because of what Sanders accurately called those "damned emails." Indeed, we would probably be even more depressed in at least one respect. Were Clinton president, we would be looking forward, as it were, only to an electoral bloodbath in 2018 and further victories by the Republican right. And 2020 would feature a bevy of eager Republican candidates, some of them offering a more palatable version of Trump, some of them from the admirable "Never Trump" wing like Ohio governor John Kasich, eager to challenge either a seventy-four-year-old incumbent with few, if any, achievements, or a Democrat who had mounted a divisive primary challenge to the incumbent. Now it is Democrats who are understandably energized and looking forward to the 2018 midterms and the 2020 general election, while Republicans are almost desperate to pass their maximalist agenda right now for fear that they won't be in full control after the voters speak in only sixteen months.

But my central point is that even if Democrats come back in 2018 and 2020, it is unlikely that all the planets will converge to allow the passage of truly progressive programs. And one, even if not the only, reason is the risk of dangerous dysfunctionality built into the Constitution in 1787.

Let me return, though, to your central notion of constitutional rot. What is so striking about your analysis is the extent to which it tracks what I labeled the "Madisonian anxiety" in my book *Framed: America's 51 Constitutions and the Crisis of Governance*. The Madison especially of *Federalist* No. 10 was obsessed by the problem of "faction," i.e., the entrance into, and success within, politics of groups committed not to the "common good" but, rather, to their own narrow and selfish interests. Although much is made of the fact that Madison also was a devotee of designing a constitution that, by pitting "ambition against ambition," would minimize the ravages of factional governance, one cannot read his oeuvre without realizing that he never gave up the hope that elite leaders would in fact be willing to tame their own selfishness—and that of their constituents—in behalf of more general values and interests. At the very least, this generated deep suspicion about the value of political parties.

When I entered graduate school, now some fifty-five years ago, political parties were, by and large, praised as organizations that would manage conflict within the polity first by directing their attention toward a mythic "median voter" standing firmly in the center of the political spectrum and then, post-election, by manifesting a willingness to compromise, to engage in deal making, with those of the other party. It helped, of course, that both were in their own way "big tent" parties. The Democratic Party was an uneasy—many would say, unholy—coalition of southern white racists (some of whom were liberal so long as African Americans received no piece of the pie) and northern liberals; Republicans in turn were fiscal conservatives, anti-labor, and often, in keeping with their self-designation as "the party of Lincoln," pro–civil rights. The Civil Rights Act of 1964 would never have passed without the strong support of Republicans William McCulloch in the House of Representatives and Everett McKinley Dirksen in the Senate. (Indeed, one of the proud additions to the 2016 and subsequent edition of the constitutional law casebook that we coedited is the text of Dirksen's truly great speech in behalf of ending the record-breaking filibuster of the Civil Rights Act.) Paradoxically or not, the Voting Rights Act of 1965 destroyed the existing Democratic coalition and led to the migration of white racists to a Republican Party that was, using suitably coded language, happy to accept them. Median voters may continue to exist in the minds of political scientists, but they play precious little role in the electoral strategies of either of the now-base-driven political parties, especially at the congressional level, where only a bit more than 10 percent of the 435 House districts can be said to be truly "competitive." The only election that really counts in the overwhelming majority of districts is the party primary, where the truly relevant "median voter" is firmly ensconced within a given party and not an outsider genuinely mulling over which political party to vote for.

"Compromise," especially within the Republican Party, has become an epithet; nor, in candor, do many contemporary Democrats wish their champions to bend over backward in cooperation with a despised Republican congressional majority. I supported the filibuster of Justice Gorsuch's nomination to the Supreme Court, even as I knew it would be fruitless, because I saw no reason for the Democrats to be "good sports" with regard to stealing the seat that might well/should have gone to Merrick Garland. Nor am I eager to see Democrats collaborate with Donald Trump in any important respect that would allow him to brag of some "achievement" should he run for reelection in 2020. Mitch McConnell was completely rational in declaring that his goal was to make Barack Obama a one-term president, which meant trying to torpedo all of his legislative goals. That he failed does not invalidate his aim. The problem is not that McConnell was a vigorous opponent of Obama; it is, instead, that the Constitution makes it so very difficult to achieve a genuine governing coalition that can, well, govern.

But another point about the sensibility of political scientists a half-century ago is worth mentioning: I think it is fair to say that there was an overwhelming culture of skepticism about the operational meaning and value of such terms as "the public interest" or "the common good." Political theory, it was often asserted, was "dead." There was simply no reason for political scientists to waste their time on the endless and irresolvable disputes among Plato, Hobbes, Locke, Rousseau, Kant, Mill, and Marx, to mention only some of the denizens of the Western political tradition. Instead, an interest-group theory of politics—about which you have written so tellingly in much of your own work—dominated. Whatever turned out to be the vector sum of the interaction among the various interest groups was simply defined as "the public interest," not least because, as the product of compromise, it might produce social stability and stave off threatened disorder. But woe unto any naïve student who argued that some particular agreement, however widely supported by various interest groups, in fact contravened "the public interest." Who in the world could supply concrete meaning to that evanescent term? It was, at best, yet another essentially contested concept. At worst, it was simply a marker laid down in a barrage of propaganda in which one's own favorite interest groups were described as instantiations of the public interest, while one's opponents were selfish factionalists. But the cognoscenti were much too sophisticated to take such language truly seriously, even if it might be useful in political campaigns directed at a naïve citizenry.

To some extent, the situation changed in 1971, with the revival of political theory generated by the publication of John Rawls's *A Theory of Justice*, though theorists identified with Leo Strauss at the University of Chicago had certainly been more than willing to criticize the model of "value-free" social science that then dominated the academy. Rawls scarcely reigned supreme, however. By 1974 Robert Nozick counterattacked with *Anarchy, State, and Utopia*. Even sophisticates started talking once more about what might constitute a public interest, though they also had to contend with the great work of Kenneth Arrow and other devotees of social choice theory who certainly provided no reason for confidence in the ability of "democratic institutions" to achieve it. In any event, I think that development of the notion of constitutional rot will require guidance in how we genuinely can tell the difference between those representatives and would-be leaders who are truly committed to achieving the common good as against those who are not.

This requires a different argument, incidentally, from one that emphasizes the breakdown of genuine "representation" in favor of rule by oligarchs, who are able to use their financial power, including the ability to fund campaigns, to render nearly irrelevant the wishes of the mass public. (Thus your argument about Donald Trump's betrayal of the hopes and wishes of much of his base, who scarcely support the collapse of the American welfare state.) It is one thing to criticize the American political system, quite deservedly, as insufficiently democratic or in thrall to moneyed interests. But it is quite another to assume that even a more "democratic" and fairly financed system would generate policies that genuinely serve the public interest rather than feed the maws of groups within the majority coalition. That was, after all, the basis for Madison's anxiety and the critique of democracy by his eighteenth-century republican counterparts.

And, dare I suggest, a full analysis of constitutional rot will require wrestling with one of the truly central figures in American legal history, Oliver Wendell Holmes. He delivered the most important single speech on American law in our history, an 1897 address to Boston University students entitled "The Path of the Law." He introduced the notion of the "bad man" as a useful heuristic to understand the actual operation of the law. The "bad man," Holmes suggested—and one might recall that in the same speech he declared that the future of the law belonged to the economist and statistician, and most certainly not to the traditional analyst of legal doctrine—was a parody of "economic man," concerned exclusively with maximizing his own interests and, therefore, treating the abstractions of the law only as setting a "price" for disobedience. If the price is relatively insubstantial, then it is always rational for the "bad man" to ignore the law, paying the price if need be, and attaining his instrumental objective.

To be sure, there is something illuminating about Holmes's analysis, which instantiates his own willingness to wash pietistic verities about the rule of law in what he famously called the "cynical acid" of actuality. That being said, one might nonetheless view the "bad man" as in fact a "*bad* man," unless, that is, one comes to the independent judgment, based on a complex moral and political theory, that the laws being disdained and ignored by the putative "bad man" are in fact bad themselves. But Holmes made no such argument, nor has that been taken to be his message by future generations of law students, lawyers, and their teachers in the legal academy. Instead, the legal academy—including, certainly, its most elite outposts—in effect teaches students to assume that their clients are simply devoted to what Madison would have termed "factious" enterprises and that it is the lawyer's duty to do whatever is legally permissible to further the client's goals. Down that road lies the notion of the client as little more than a sociopath and the lawyer as his enabler within very broad limits. Down that road, one might say, lies Donald Trump, who truly epitomizes, in every conceivable way, the psychology of the Holmesian "bad man" and who is able to purchase lawyers who are apparently eager to use the tools of their trade to defend what is in fact dishonorable conduct.

Trump reveals another reality of the law and of legal education. In our "professional responsibility" courses, we tend to focus on the moral issues raised by lawyers charged with defending those accused of criminal misconduct. I have relatively little trouble defending vigorous advocacy in behalf of even "obviously guilty" clients, because it is important, as you indeed suggest, to have an independent bar that attempts to keep the state honest, as it were, when revving up what is sometimes the awful machinery of state power against those it deems criminal. But Trump has not, so far as I am aware, been charged with criminal offenses; instead, he is a chronic cheat who has been the defendant, apparently, in literally hundreds of civil lawsuits, ranging from breach of contract to the fraud that was Trump University. His lawyers are under no duty to provide him with vigorous defenses; rather, they choose to collaborate with the quintessential "bad man" because he pays well (assuming he doesn't try to stiff his lawyers the way he stiffs others who do business with him). One suspects that none of his lawyers has ever for a single instant adopted the view of the American Bar Association, in its own Model Code of Professional Responsibility, that lawyers should engage in conversation with their clients about the morality of their conduct, even if, by stipulation, they have a legal right to behave like louts. Nor is there any record of lawyers publicly walking away from Trump because his odious conduct tarnishes them as well. After all, we teach our students that one should not judge lawyers by the clients they choose to serve, since everyone deserves the best lawyering that money can buy.

Just as Donald Trump should cause all of us to reassess at least aspects of our constitutional law courses on, say, presidential power, so should the reality of a "bad man" like Donald Trump as president force us to revisit Holmes and ask what the consequences are of facilely accepting the "bad man" as the template for clients and then the lawyers who defend them. Perhaps we should recall John Dean's famous testimony before the Watergate Committee, when he was asked why he placed asterisks next to the names of certain Nixon administration officials. His answer was that they were all lawyers, who might, in a better world, have been expected to draw the line at many of Nixon's requests. Indeed, a direct result of Dean's testimony was the decision by the ABA to require enhanced education of law students in the requirements of professional responsibility. One may, of course, wonder about the actual impact of such courses, assuming they are even offered. Your own Yale Law School is well-known for claiming to teach the subject "pervasively" by ostensibly raising professional responsibility questions in every course rather than requiring a separate course devoted to the subject. One might well wonder about the actual effectiveness of this approach.

In any event, the concept of constitutional rot is both valuable and extremely disturbing if one takes it fully seriously. We are fighting a multi-front battle at the present time. One of the striking realities of at least some contemporary literature is its willingness to express near contempt for the possibility of intelligent "reflection and choice" on the part of the public, which one would think is a predicate condition for taking democracy seriously. This is the central theme of Ilya Somin's important book *Democracy and Political Ignorance*, which borrows from the arguments of many economists that it is simply "irrational" to expect that ordinary voters will devote enough time and energy actually to studying issues before casting their ballots. Somin, a principled libertarian committed to "smaller government," consistently castigated Donald Trump, though he could scarcely have been surprised that millions of ignorant voters would choose to follow the demagogue down the primrose path. One might say much the same about our friend Randy Barnett, whose recent book *Our Republican Constitution* is also strikingly disdainful of democracy. But both Somin and Barnett, not to mention many other very smart conservatives like Michael Greve or Richard Epstein, certainly have no reluctance to articulate strong views of what "the public interest" requires. Indeed, Barnett appears to adopt the language of classic natural law and natural rights. To defeat them, one must develop substantive theories of "the public interest" or "common good" that will withstand their often formidable critiques. Indeed, a common theme of some recent punditry is that Democrats must develop and articulate genuinely attractive public policies and not rely on the "mere" fact that Donald Trump is an ignoramus who threatens our collective future.

One further aspect of your analysis is worth mentioning. You emphasize the contemporary significance of polarization and what might be termed the "Otherization"—and demonization—of political opponents. But surely this is nothing new in our politics. One has only to read the heated rhetoric surrounding the 1800 presidential election to realize that Madison's naïve hopes of 1787 were almost totally mistaken. Parties were destined to become part of the American political fabric. But this meant, practically speaking, that many Federalists deemed Jefferson to be the satanic anti-Christ because of his support of the French Revolution; Jeffersonians returned the compliment by viewing Adams as the lackey of elite toffs determined to maintain their class superiority. And Alexander Hamilton, who had little use for Jefferson, nonetheless supported him over Aaron Burr after the fiasco of the tied electoral vote because he had utter contempt for Burr's political character. Indeed, I published an op-ed in May 2016 quoting from Hamilton's denunciations of Burr, which track to an astonishing degree what many would say of Donald Trump, and suggested that honorable Republicans should emulate Hamilton by supporting Hillary Clinton, the Jefferson analogue. Nor can one read the imprecations directed against Abraham Lincoln in 1860 and believe that the past was a time of concord.

There have always been deep divisions within the American polity, and there have been recurrent challenges to the ability of the formal constitutional system to contain those divisions. And, to put it mildly, there have not always been happy endings with regard to these challenges. I suspect both of us believe that the "rot" you identify, whether or not a "crisis" of the constitutional order, will continue and provide a necessary context for our discussions.

Sandy

AUGUST 29, 2017

Dear Sandy,

My last letter offered a theory about constitutional rot in the American political system. In this letter, I want to connect the idea of constitutional rot to my analysis of political time.

The progress of constitutional rot in the United States is inextricably linked to the rise and fall of the Republican Party, because that party, despite its many troubles, remains the dominant political party in the country, and the opposition party—the Democrats—has so far been unable to shake it from its dominant status. Even in opposition, congressional Republicans have been remarkably effective. They mastered and deployed the arts of gridlock and political obstruction to great effect. To give only one example, there would have been no Debt Ceiling Crisis in 2011 and no government shutdowns in 1995, 2013 [and 2018!] without their intransigence.

Moreover, because the Republican Party controls most if not all of the levers of power in the national government, it is the only political party that can effectively stand up to and check Trump's misbehavior and breaches of political and constitutional norms—even though, to this point, Republican leaders have proved unwilling to do so. Quite the contrary: Many of them seem more than happy to protect Trump and shield him from the many investigations and scandals swirling around him.

[Steven Levitsky and Daniel Ziblatt's book *How Democracies Die*, published after these letters were written, emphasizes the crucial role of political parties—and especially conservative political parties—in checking demagogues and protecting democratic norms from would-be autocrats. Unless party leaders are willing to display political courage to protect democratic norms, Levitsky and Ziblatt argue, democracies can slowly perish. This makes the role of Republican political leaders especially crucial. (As Levitsky and Ziblatt point out, these leaders failed to keep Trump from gaining the Republican nomination in the first place.) Even after the 2016 election, Republican leaders remain the most effective check on Trump in a unified government.

However, as I argued in my letter of December 3, 2016, the very features of political polarization perfected in the Reagan regime have bound Republican leaders ever more tightly to Trump. They fear standing up to him because they fear alienating their own base of Republican voters, who seem remarkably happy with Trump's no-nothing populism and reality-show authoritarianism. Years of stoking populist rage for short-term political gain have left Republican leaders fearful of crossing their constituents by opposing their voters' politically incorrect hero, Donald Trump. The only Republican political leaders who have been willing to criticize Trump are those who are already out of politics or who are about to retire. The behavior of Republicans who are actually in power has hardly been a profile in courage. Some have been unprincipled accommodators; others spineless sycophants.

It is unlikely that the Republican Party's political leaders will move to check Trump—including challenging him in the presidential primaries—until after the party has been soundly defeated in the 2018 elections. They would act then because of the danger that Trump will lead them to even more disastrous results in 2020. Their political courage, in other words, is unlikely to revive until goaded by their political self-interest and their desire for political survival. And if my predictions prove correct, even standing up to Trump at that late hour will not be sufficient to prevent the dissolution of the Reagan regime and the emergence of a new political regime led by the opposite party.]

It may be hard to credit the larger narrative of political time I have been presenting in these letters, because Trump currently bestrides the news cycle like a colossus. A master manipulator and con artist, he appears to be driving the story of American politics. He has cowed the electoral leaders of his party into submission. He seems to presage a new populist and nativist era in politics—leading a loyal political base and a conservative party reorganized around his values. But appearances can be deceiving. Like Hoover and Carter before him, Trump is not the master of the situation; he is actually at the mercy of forces well beyond his ability to control. He has not ended the processes of decay in his party's coalition; if anything, he has accelerated them.

Donald Trump's Two Tracks

Donald Trump's presidency has operated on two tracks. First, Trump has continued to issue deregulatory orders, and undermine environmental protection and labor regulation, while appointing reliably conservative federal judges who have been recommended by conservative think tanks and key figures in the Federalist Society. Trump also supported the repeal of Obamacare and the congressional Republican plan for slashing taxes on the wealthy. Operating on this track, Trump is largely indistinguishable from a very conservative Republican politician.

The second track is where Trump has gotten the most attention. In this mode, he has flamboyantly played to his base of supporters through techniques of cultural warfare, xenophobia, and white identity politics. He has engaged in a seemingly endless stream of populist and racially inflammatory actions and statements. He has threatened trade wars and picked fights with traditional allies, thumping his chest and proclaiming that he won't let other countries take advantage of the U.S.

In the process, he has attacked many of his fellow Republicans. But that is not because he is thinking of leaving the Republican Party. Quite the contrary—he is already running for reelection. Rather, it is because he is laying claim to control of the party.

Polls indicate that Trump's national approval rating has declined by about a percentage point a month since his inauguration [and now appears to have stabilized at around 40 to 42 percent]. Nevertheless, Trump still remains far more popular than most members of Congress. And as long as he remains popular among the Republican faithful, it is almost impossible for the vast majority of Republicans—even those he attacks—to disown him. As noted previously, it will probably take a major defeat in the 2018 elections—or incontrovertible evidence of impeachable offenses—to cause Republican politicians to defect from him. And even then, Republicans risk alienating Trump's sizable group of loyal Republican followers.

As the Republican legislative agenda has stalled, Trump has repeatedly turned to the second track—creating one cultural controversy after another to distract, discomfit, and exacerbate political polarization and mutual distrust among the citizenry. By this point in his presidency, much of Trump's political strategy has been reduced to a series of radical gestures that please his populist base, no matter how much they may outrage the rest of the country. Indeed, he welcomes the scorn and calumny of his political opponents: the more outrageous his speech and actions, the more he signals that he is standing up to the globalists and the elites—and that he is on the side of the real Americans.

Overhanging all of this is the continuing investigation into the relationship between Trump, his associates, and Russia. As the evidence slowly mounts, Trump acts more and more like a person who has something to hide, and who knows that the authorities are getting closer and closer to discovering it. He not only attacks the press; he also lashes out at his own Justice Department, intelligence services, and the FBI—lying shamelessly and extravagantly, and driving his base to distrust every institution of civil society or government that might oppose or expose him.

Political Dysfunction in a Unitary Government

When you and I wrote about political dysfunction during the Obama years, Sandy, we assumed that a significant cause of dysfunction was divided government combined with intense political polarization.

But that is not the case today. Throughout his presidency, Trump has had the advantage of Republican majorities in both houses of Congress and a Republican majority on the Supreme Court. And yet political dysfunction at the national level is as bad as the last four years of the Obama administration—perhaps even worse. Congressional Republicans are operating the government through a series of short-term spending bills, moving from deadline to deadline, with no apparent policy objectives other than finding yet another way to lower taxes on their wealthy donors.

If Trump and his party have been ineffective, it is not because of divided government. After all, when the Democrats controlled the White House and both houses of Congress between 2009 and 2010, they got a great deal accomplished. Rather, the dysfunction is due to other, deeper causes—in particular, the gradual exhaustion of the Republican coalition.

Coalitions decline and fall when their agenda becomes irrelevant to the problems that the country faces, and when their constituent parts factionalize and turn on each other. In some cases, the coalition may be the victim of its own success. Its solutions—and its ideological agenda—may be causes of the problems the country faces. The New Deal coalition unraveled in the tumult of the late 1960s and 1970s; something structurally similar is happening to the Reagan coalition today.

The Reagan coalition came together on a mission to deregulate the economy, shrink the size of government, and above all lower taxes, especially on the wealthy. This formula has proved inadequate in responding to current social problems, no matter how strong the party appears at present. In the long run, the disconnect between Republican ideology and public expectations is unsustainable.

The failed attempt to repeal Obamacare in the summer of 2017 exemplifies the problem. The American public had gradually come to view access to health care and affordable health insurance as part of the social contract—something the government should work to guarantee. This assumes, however, a vision of government deeply at odds with the ideological assumptions of the contemporary Republican Party. It is especially at odds with the desires and interests of the donor class who support Republican politicians and drive the party's agenda. Obamacare secured access to health care through redistribution—it raised taxes on investment income; and it grew government entitlements—through insurance subsidies and the expansion of Medicaid. No wonder that Reaganite true believers despised it.

Even so, congressional Republicans could not repeal Obamacare because they never reached a consensus on what to do instead. They never reached a consensus because what most of them actually wanted to do was deeply unpopular—hack away at Medicaid and deregulate the insurance industry in order to pay for tax cuts for wealthy Americans. What most congressional Republicans really wanted, in other words, was yet another version of the post-1980 Republican policy agenda—to cut entitlements and alleviate fiscal and regulatory burdens on the donor class. As the saying goes, when all that you have is a hammer, everything—including your solution to health policy—looks like a nail.

At the same time, Republicans—and Trump himself—promised something very different to the public. They repeatedly blamed Obamacare for raising premiums and limiting access to health care. They promised that their plan—never fully specified—would lower premiums and extend access to health care for more people. In fact, all of their plans would have done the opposite—leaving tens of millions without health insurance and raising rates for the elderly and the sick. To keep the Reagan coalition running, in short, Republicans engaged in demagoguery on the health care issue for years and repeatedly misled the public about what they would do. Eventually, the piper had to be paid.

I emphasize these points because no matter whom the Republicans nominated in 2016, they would have faced this dilemma. It is unlikely that Presidents Ted Cruz, Marco Rubio, or Jeb Bush could have resolved the central problems facing the Reagan regime and the Republican coalition. They would have faced a fractious party with radicalized elements, with each faction demanding that things be done their way or not at all. They would have faced a deep disconnect between what the public thought it was getting in health care reform and what the donor class—and therefore Republican politicians—were planning to give them.

Quite apart from Trump's incompetence, the Senate filibuster rules and the House's Hastert Rule have hampered Republican ambitions. Republicans are forced to pass legislation with only Republican votes, giving them little room for error, and making it possible for a small number of representatives and senators to hold up passage in the service of conflicting and contradictory demands.

He Who Lives by Demagoguery and Obstruction
Shall Die by Demagoguery and Obstruction

The difficulties that Republicans faced in pushing their agenda through Congress might seem wholly unrelated to the emergence of a racist, ignorant demagogue as the political leader of the Republican Party. But both of them are connected to the forces that produced the rise and fall of the Reagan regime.

The Reagan regime kept itself in power by combining its deregulatory and tax-cutting policies—which primarily favored elite donors—

with anti-elitist rhetoric, white identity politics, and strategies of political polarization.

Republicans repeatedly found cultural wedge issues and symbolic crusades to anger their base and focus them on issues of culture and white identity. Republicans created a world in which Democrats were, as Newt Gingrich once said of Bill Clinton, "the enemy of normal Americans." Republicans created a world in which Barack Obama, a neoliberal policy wonk, was portrayed as an alien anti-colonialist radical born in Kenya and secretly set on the destruction of the United States. Republican media inundated their listeners with propaganda and disinformation, convincing the base that liberals and Democrats could never be trusted, and that at heart they were evil, stupid, alien, and traitorous.

These devices were enormously successful: they kept the Reagan coalition together far longer than it perhaps deserved. But these strategies of polarization and diversion had an unfortunate side effect: they created and fueled a strongly ideological, angry, anti-elitist Republican base that increasingly despised all compromise with Democrats and liberals, and embraced populist con artists like Newt Gingrich and Rush Limbaugh, who, in turn, paved the way for populist demagogues like Sarah Palin and Donald Trump. Indeed, when John McCain chose the egregiously unqualified Palin as his running mate in order to shore up support with an increasingly angry Republican base, it was a sign that the Grand Old Party had begun to undermine itself.

The same strategies of political polarization led to the procedural roadblocks that hamper Republicans today. Thirty years ago, the Senate's filibuster rules and related procedural devices were far less important than they are today. That changed after Republicans began using them in the 1990s to hinder Bill Clinton. The emergence of the informal Hastert Rule, which limits the House, is a product of the same era. It promotes ideological purity by preventing Republicans from defecting and forming bipartisan coalitions with Democrats.

Intransigence and obstruction made some sense politically. They helped safeguard against redistribution and new regulations; they also helped Republicans fight the culture wars. Democrats predictably responded during George W. Bush's presidency, most notably, by filibustering a series of circuit court appointments. By the time Barack Obama entered the White House, Senate Minority (now Majority)

Leader Mitch McConnell had made political obstruction—and the sixty-vote threshold in the Senate—a standard feature of national politics. Moreover, conservative populist ideology—its visceral distrust of elites, and what Skowronek has called its perpetual war on the policy state[1]—made it difficult for Republican politicians to legislate effectively when they finally gained power. They were especially good at blocking, smearing, and blowing things up. They were less well trained for other political tasks.

In this way, Republican political strategies have sown the seeds of the party's political destruction. Polarization and populism have produced a politics of stupidity *and* dysfunction, a politics in which a Republican demagogue in the White House oversees a Republican-controlled Congress that has great difficulty enacting its agenda.

It still remains likely that Republicans will conveniently cast aside their dire warnings about deficits—which resurface whenever Democrats are in power—and pass a budget-busting tax cut for their donors, as they did during George W. Bush's first term. After all, if congressional Republicans cannot lower taxes for their donor class, they have almost no reason for existing as a party. Beyond this, however, they seem impotent and internally divided.

Political Strategies of a Dying Regime— Constrict the Electorate, Stock Up on Judges

When regimes sense that they are losing power, they react in predictable ways. They try to increase the voting power of their likely supporters, and they try to decrease the voting power of their likely opponents. This is a central reason for the Republican strategy of vote suppression, which Republicans have justified publicly by specious claims of voter fraud. The real motivation, however, for a host of vote-suppression measures—ranging from voter ID laws to moving or closing polling places—is to decrease the effective size of the electorate and make it more friendly to Republicans. A Republican-appointed majority on the U.S. Supreme Court helped matters along in 2013 by crippling the preclearance provisions of the Voting Rights

---

1. Stephen Skowronek, "Twentieth-Century Remedies," *Boston University Law Review* 94 (2014): 804.

Act in *Shelby County v. Holder*.[2] Chief Justice Roberts solemnly intoned that things have changed in the South and federal supervision was no longer necessary. Republican state governments, both in and out of the South, took this as a cue to restrict the franchise even more.

In addition to constricting the suffrage, a regime in decline will increasingly turn to the federal judiciary to defend its values from its opponents and push its policies through constitutional and statutory interpretation. It is therefore no wonder that the one thing Republicans were able to agree on was the necessity of keeping President Obama from filling Justice Antonin Scalia's seat on the Supreme Court. It is also no wonder that Senate Majority Leader Mitch McConnell, the champion of the filibuster and master of political obstruction, was willing to jettison the filibuster for Supreme Court appointments in order to push through Neil Gorsuch's appointment to replace Scalia, and maintain a conservative majority on the Court.

As a regime matures and declines, one of its most important tasks is to stock the federal judiciary with life-tenured judges friendly to the regime's commitments of ideology and interest. Judges can serve as a bulwark to defend the regime's values in the days ahead, using the power of judicial review to protect those commitments when they are threatened.

The modern conservative movement grew to maturity attacking judicial review, which they identified with the liberal decisions of the 1960s and 1970s. Now, in the dog days of the crumbling Reagan regime, many conservatives regard robust judicial review—or judicial engagement, as it is now called—as an important obligation of the federal judiciary.

* * *

Donald Trump is the most obvious symbol—and product—of the decadence of the Reagan regime as it teeters toward its eventual collapse. He is a political menace who should never have been elected in the first place. But the reason he rose to power owes much to the decay of the Republican Party he leads.

Like many Americans, I would be delighted to remove Trump from the presidency before his term expires. But he is the symptom and

2. 570 U.S. 529 (2013).

not the cause of our current dysfunction. Removing Trump cannot fix what ails the Republican Party. The angry base it created, the fractious, radicalized party, the demagogic media, the echo chamber of propaganda, will all remain. Even if Donald Trump were to vanish tomorrow, replaced by Mike Pence, Republicans would face many of the same problems they face today. The head stinks, but it sits atop a rotten corpse.

Jack

PART FIVE

EXECUTIVE POWER
AND CONSTITUTIONAL
DICTATORSHIP

OCTOBER 7, 2017

Dear Jack,

I've tarried a bit in responding to your earlier letter, which is perilous given our current situation. So much happens, so quickly. Many new events have piled up that could call for comment.

I think it is relevant to the theme of our overall conversation—and your important notion of constitutional rot as a clear and present danger to the survival of our constitutional order—to note that in a course I am teaching at the Harvard Law School this semester on *The Federalist*, the conversation turned to whether there are any genuine heroes among national-level political leaders. What kicked this off was Publius's offering as an independent reason for ratifying the Constitution the fact that it was drafted by obviously estimable persons in Philadelphia, the most notable of whom, of course, was George Washington. Whether or not they were wearing togas, one could detect in at least some of them a genuine commitment to serving their country and not simply their crass private interests. So I asked the students whether they perceive any similar persons on the present stage. The only contemporary who was mentioned by any of the dozen or so students in my reading course was McCain, because, at least on several occasions, he has displayed genuine, seemingly selfless, integrity.

Perhaps one can argue that a truly mature political system has no need for "heroes"; competence and trustworthiness should be enough. But I do think that we'd like to believe that people making decisions concerning matters of life and death, peace and war, or access to health care are at least somewhat exceptional in a capacity to demonstrate what Hemingway notably called "grace under pressure" (a catchphrase picked up by Kennedy acolytes to describe their champion). In the contemporary world, this could be demonstrated by standing up to donors and other financiers of modern political campaigns or, somewhat similarly, standing up to the demands of single-issue groups who can credibly threaten to turn out their supporters in an election. Interestingly enough, McCain in a 2002 memoir regretted what he himself termed his "coward[ice]" in capitulating to unreconstructed southern whites during the 2000 South Carolina Republican primary and refusing to denounce the flying of the Confederate flag on the state Capitol grounds. Of course, if that had enabled him to beat the even more craven George W. Bush, perhaps he would have described that, however ruefully, as simply the kind of compromise one has to make to succeed in a fallen political world. As Michael Walzer has notably argued, to participate seriously in politics inevitably requires a willingness to dirty one's hands.

The federal government's handling of Hurricane Maria is especially troubling. It is likely to be of long-term importance because of its devastation of Puerto Rico and Puerto Rico's peculiar constitutional status. The Supreme Court in 1901 held in effect that the United States could, like Britain, France, and Germany, be a genuine imperial power and gain new territories without any obligation to treat them as genuinely part of the greater polity. Most notably, the Court held that Puerto Rico was not "within the United States" constitutionally. Though Puerto Ricans are citizens, thanks to the Jones Act of 1917, Puerto Ricans on the island (unlike the majority of Puerto Ricans who now live on the mainland and, therefore, can vote in their new states of residence) are very much at the mercy of Congress and the president with regard to many of their practical political rights. Puerto Rico has no voting representation whatsoever in Congress; nor, unlike Washington, D.C., is Puerto Rico able to cast any electoral votes for the presidency. There are few political incentives genuinely to care about Puerto Rico.

It would certainly not surprise me if sentiment in Puerto Rico moved more solidly toward a desire toward statehood (or, in contrast, independence). The present "commonwealth" status has exhibited its limitations. What if the roughly 45 percent of contemporary Puerto Ricans who wish for statehood within the United States becomes transformed into a solid majority? Article IV of the Constitution leaves it up to Congress as to whether or not to admit new states. So what would Congress do? Some representatives and senators would undoubtedly be apoplectic at the prospect of a state that has Spanish as its dominant, indeed "official," language. Others, whether they would speak entirely candidly, would be apoplectic at the prospect of seven additional electoral votes—Puerto Rico is roughly the population of Connecticut—that would be extremely likely to go to Democratic candidates, not to speak, of course, of the five new likely Democratic representatives and two new likely Democratic senators.

This would be an episode of "constitutional politics" in its most obvious sense. If Congress were to reject statehood, then one might well envision that the pro-independence party, which currently has less than 10 percent support, would skyrocket. Few persons in 1770, after all, would really have predicted the American secession of 1776. It took almost literally incredibly stupid British decisions, beginning with their over-response to the Boston Tea Party in 1773, to create the circumstances whereby the almost certain minority of committed "American patriots" could embark on an ultimately successful secessionist insurrection. Other issues, like the one to which I will turn in the next paragraph, are more pressing as we write, but it would be foolhardy to ignore the potential magnitude for anyone interested in American constitutional development, both in theory and practice, of recent events in Puerto Rico.

But there can be little doubt that in the six weeks since your last letter, the threat of war with North Korea, possibly involving the use of nuclear weapons, looms ever more threateningly on the horizon. It might take us too far afield to engage in a full-scale discussion of North Korea. But let me say that I view North Korea as a completely rational regime that has incorporated the lessons of what might be called Deterrence Theory 101: If one is faced with a hegemonic adversary threatening the basic existence of the regime, then the rational response is to develop weapons sufficient to deter an attack by engaging in a credible threat to the hegemon itself.

As you know, I have recently written a book on why it is of some value to read *The Federalist* in the twenty-first century. One of the reasons is provided by *Federalist* No. 11, which I'm quite confident is never read save by specialists. But in it Publius emphasizes the various national security threats to the nascent United States and the necessity of creating a government strong enough to build an effective navy for the purpose of fending off predictable attacks (and, in addition, protecting American commerce). I suspect that Chinese and North Korean readers of *The Federalist* would find this lesson very compatible. I am not in the least afraid that North Korea would engage in a gratuitous attack on the United States or, indeed, its allies South Korea and Japan. That would truly be irrational, since they have to be aware that the United States could (and would) in fact obliterate North Korea. But like many both home and abroad, I am more fearful of Donald Trump than of Kim Jong-un. Neither, to be sure, is a model of leadership, but I find our own president far more unpredictable and unstable, in every way.

I've adverted to *Federalist* No. 11 as a possible source of insight into understanding the behavior of China and North Korea. But perhaps more important for our discussion is *Federalist* No. 8, where Publius says that a major reason to ratify the Constitution is to avoid becoming a militarized society. His argument goes like this: If the fractious states unite behind a strong central government that would, among other things, be enabled to create a standing army, then that, plus the sheer fact that we would be protected by the great pond of the Atlantic Ocean, would assure us a relatively pacific future. If, on the other hand, opponents of the Constitution prevailed, and we divided into two or three separate countries along the Atlantic Coast, then endless war would be likely, and the civic culture would rapidly be transformed from the benevolent commercial one that Publius endorsed into a militaristic one because of the equally endless fear of war and the need to support armies and navies sufficient to defend oneself. Just as importantly, we would valorize what might be called the "military virtues" instead of what we learned to call the "bourgeois virtues" attached with seeking individual economic success.

Since World War II, at the latest, we have lost that sense of isolationist protection against would-be adversaries. The Atlantic long since lost its status as a secure barrier once the Soviet Union developed ICBMs that could attack the homeland. And now we discover that the even vaster Pacific might not be adequate either. Interestingly enough, our panic is over a country that poses no rational existential threat to the United States, unlike, say, China, which might be developing, for example, a far more secure nuclear arsenal. In any event, it is especially important to have at the helm as president somebody in whom we repose some degree of genuine trust, based on a mixture of relevant knowledge and a demonstrated capacity for measured and temperate decision making. Donald Trump fails on all conceivable counts.

But it gets even worse. As Stephen Griffin has argued, since World War II and, especially, Harry Truman's unilateral decision to go to war in Korea in 1950, we have seemingly placed more and more power in the hands of the president. It is now regarded as simply naïve to point to the text of the Constitution and its assignment to Congress of the power to "declare war." How old-fashioned! Instead, one can turn even to NPR, that ostensible bastion of liberal political sensibilities, and hear it said, almost laconically, that the decision whether to go to war against North Korea is in the hands of Donald Trump alone. That is, he needs no declaration of war; it's not even clear, according to some of these savants, that he needs Congress to pass a formal Authorization for Use of Military Force.

George H. W. Bush, in seeking such an authorization in 1991, prior to invading Iraq, was careful to indicate that he regarded it basically as a courtesy—or an attempt to build up political support—rather than a constitutional necessity. Barack Obama notably engaged in acts of war against Libya, a country that constituted no threat to the United States, without gaining congressional approval, and at one point it appeared that he might attack Syria on his own. (We know that he authorized drone strikes in various places around the world in countries with whom we were not at war or where the targets could not plausibly be described as architects of the September 11 attacks.) Our friends and colleagues Bruce Ackerman and Marty Lederman, among others, have certainly pushed back against this exaggerated understanding of presidential authority, but I fear that that battle has been fundamentally lost. Ironically or not, "popular constitutionalism"—something that both of us are intensely interested in and, to a significant degree, support—has seemingly made its peace with what we called in one of the articles we coauthored "constitutional dictatorship."

We noted that there is a distinguished lineage of political theorists, going back at least to Machiavelli, who in turn was writing about ancient Rome, who argued in behalf of including such a possibility within any well-designed constitution. But we also noted, citing in particular the late political scientist Clinton Rossiter, that the United States has a particularly poor version of such a dictatorship, especially with regard to the use of military force. I believe that the key event was John Kennedy's actions during the Cuban Missile Crisis, about which I am a decided revisionist, against the general tendency to laud those thirteen days as Kennedy's finest hour and a precedent for future presidential unilateralism.

Ironically, the War Powers Act, passed during the Nixon administration in an ostensible attempt to rein in presidential power, has instead seemingly become, in practice, a permission slip for the president to initiate hostilities for sixty days without having to worry about receiving any congressional permission. And, of course, Yale's own former dean, Harold Koh, offered a notably crabbed interpretation of what "hostilities" mean that suggested that so long as the United States is only threatening the lives of foreigners and not putting American armed forces personnel at risk, then the War Powers Act doesn't apply at all. One might note that Donald Trump has said not a word about putting thousands more American boots on the ground in Korea; instead, he seems to be threatening bombing from on high (as would presumably also be the case in Iran should he decide to renege on the Iran deal and move directly against that country).

One of the distinct attributes of the Trump administration is the degree to which Trump has surrounded himself with military personnel. The most important examples, of course, are his relatively new chief of staff, former marine general John F. Kelly; his national security advisor, army general H. R. McMaster, who remained in active service [prior to his dismissal in April 2018 and succession by John Bolton]; and Secretary of Defense James Mattis, another retired marine general. With regard to Mattis, Congress had to agree to a special waiver of the law prohibiting recently retired military personnel from occupying that particular office, given concerns going back to the founding about the importance of civilian control of the military. But it is a sign of the times that many political liberals are grateful about the presence and influence of the generals. We are far from the day of *Dr. Strangelove*, which satirized, among others, Curtis LeMay and other generals eager to go to war. There may still be military officials—I suspect located largely, like LeMay, in the air force—who are a bit quick to pull triggers, but the contemporary military seems to be a model of sobriety and caution. It would take us too far afield to discuss the role of torture in the conduct of the Global War on Terrorism, but there seems widespread agreement that civilians were far more prone to justify its use than were members of the uniformed military and their lawyers.

You recall, I am sure, that then-colonel Charles Dunlap speculated back in 1992 about an imagined future military coup in "The Origins of the American Military Coup of 2012," generated in part by the disillusionment of military leaders with the state of American society and the demonstrable incapacity of civilian leaders to deal effectively with the problems facing us. One might wonder if we are seeing one form of such a coup, which requires not overthrow, but simply the greater and greater entry into high positions of leadership of military leaders in whom the rest of us have more confidence than purported "leaders" picked by the electoral process (which is more and more controlled by big money and single-issue factions). Polls show that the only national institution in which the public reposes genuine "confidence" is the military. Surely this is an issue of constitutional importance, and one can be confident, *pace* Tocqueville, that the Supreme Court will have nothing at all useful to say about any such development in our constitutional order.

Even if Robert Mueller, some months from now—perhaps after this book has gone to press—sets out a bill of particulars sufficient to warrant impeachment under the most onerous burden presented by the high crimes and misdemeanors clause, that would not in the least limit Donald Trump's ability to wreak havoc in the interim. Bill Clinton remained president of the United States, with all attendant legal authority, even after he was impeached by the House of Representatives.

Indeed, one of the things I have come to despise about our constitutional order is that it leaves in power defeated incumbents for a full ten weeks after their perhaps ignominious defeats. At best, this leaves the United States without a truly functioning government; at worst, it allows the incumbents to continue making important foreign policy decisions that may affect their successors. Just think of George H. W. Bush's decision to send American troops to Somalia in December 1992. We are totally unlike the British, say, who can literally remove a prime minister overnight with a vote of "no confidence." (And it doesn't even require a vote of Parliament. As with Margaret Thatcher, the removal could be effectuated by a political party grown disillusioned with the prime minister's leadership.) To be sure, there may be a quicker alternative than impeachment, the Twenty-Fifth Amendment, but this requires, first of all, a "palace revolt," as it were, by which Trump's cabinet and vice president would take the lead in declaring that Kim Jong-un was in effect correct when describing Donald Trump as a "dotard."

What we need, and do not have, is a mechanism for instant firing via a vote of no confidence. As someone who has long advocated a new constitutional convention as a necessary pathway to much-needed (and overdue) constitutional reform, I am often asked what my single most important suggestion would be. My answer varies, in part depending on events of the day. At this time, though, I have no doubt that the answer has to do with alleviating the fixed-term presidency imposed in 1787 in favor of a process that would allow us to fire a sitting president in whom we've lost confidence.

But there is one last issue worth discussing with regard to the way we understand Donald Trump through the peculiar lens of "thinking like a constitutional lawyer." Cass Sunstein has written a tract on presidential impeachment in which he emphasizes that any proceedings against Trump must be based on scrupulously impersonal and neutral criteria. It is, he argues, simply illegitimate to offer as a rationale for impeachment that Trump lacks every characterological trait that we look for in a president, who is also, among other things, commander in chief of the contemporary U.S. armed forces. That would be, so to speak, to "personalize" impeachment, whereas lawyers should think in more general terms. Mark Graber and I have written a piece that takes issue with adhering to the entrenched tradition of "neutral principles" with regard to presidential power and, I would add, impeachment.[1] There is no good reason to treat Donald Trump as the legal equivalent of George Washington or even, if truth be known, George W. Bush. As you know, perhaps my favorite line in all of the canon is Justice John Marshall's in *McCulloch v. Maryland*: if a constitution is to endure, it must be "adapted to the various crises of human affairs." That is the basis of the "compelling interest doctrine" that allows us to deviate from strict textualism (think of the First Amendment) or well-established doctrine, as with the Court's willingness to tolerate taking race into account when a compelling interest presents itself. Usually, the compelling interest or crisis is external to the decision maker. Think of war (*Korematsu*, where Japanese American citizens

1. Sanford Levinson and Mark A. Graber, "The Constitutional Powers of Anti-Publian Presidents: Constitutional Interpretation in a Broken Constitutional Order," *Chapman Law Review* 21 (2018): 133.

and their resident-alien relatives were detained in what one justice of the Supreme Court called "concentration camps") or the Great Depression (the de facto rewriting of the contract clause in *Blaisdell* that in fact allowed Minnesota, contrary to the text of the clause, to "impair the obligation of contracts" by establishing a "moratorium" on the duty of mortgagees to pay their debts to the mortgagors). Well, the crisis we face today is the persona and frightening character of Donald Trump himself. To deny this aspect of our current situation is, I believe, to play the ostrich. We have discovered, though, that most well-trained lawyers are decidedly hesitant to leave the lofty world of neutral principles and to address the truly awful relevance of Donald Trump's particularity.

It would be, to be sure, a decidedly innovative reading of the impeachment clause to focus on character defects, as well as, to be sure, violations of the emoluments clause. But we should recognize, with suitable irony, that the original Constitution was designed to prevent a rank demagogue like Trump from occupying the presidency. The mechanism that would save us was the Electoral College! When Publius defends our bizarre method of electing presidents, in *Federalist* No. 68, it is because the electors will be trustees for the public and simply refuse to vote for a scoundrel.

> The process of election affords a moral certainty, that the office of President will never fall to the lot of any man who is not in an eminent degree endowed with the requisite qualifications. . . . It will not be too strong to say, that there will be a constant probability of seeing the station filled by characters pre-eminent for ability and virtue.

One reads these words today and weeps—or, perhaps, accepts the wisdom of James Madison in disdaining the placement of "parchment barriers" in the Constitution whose role is to be disregarded. From very early on, electors began viewing themselves simply as delegates of the particular political party to which they belonged and for whose candidate they were committed to support. We have a toxic mixture of a radically defective Constitution, which does not allow us easily, if at all, to dispose of a terrifying president, and a rotting public culture in which Donald Trump has proved capable of energizing his base by pandering to its most truly "deplorable" elements. And, so long as we are imprisoned with a legalistic approach to impeachment, we are forced to go to the country with arguments about the emoluments clause or even "obstruction of justice" rather than the far more relevant concerns about potential further calamities suggested by Trump's personal defects.

So this is how I see things on October 7. Who knows what the coming days and weeks will bring? For better or worse, we are committed to ending this epistolary exchange at the beginning of the new year, but that still gives us one more round in which we can summarize not only our changing perspectives over the past two years, when we began it, but also our reactions to whatever surprises await us in the next month. I can only hope they don't include mushroom clouds.

Sandy

NOVEMBER 6, 2017

Dear Sandy,

Congressional Republicans have pivoted from their failed attempt to repeal Obamacare to a new bill designed to reduce taxes. So far the bill appears to be a very significant reduction of taxes on wealthy people—including the president himself—paid for by an explosion of deficit spending and an increase in taxes on the middle class, as well as the reduction or elimination of many programs and tax incentives that benefit poor and middle-class Americans. [The final version of the bill also effectively repealed Obamacare's individual mandate— which required Americans to have health insurance or pay a tax—by lowering the tax for noncompliance to zero. Repealing the mandate helped finance additional tax cuts for wealthy Americans: because fewer people would insure themselves, the federal government would not have to subsidize their insurance.]

The Republican tax bill is exactly the kind of tax legislation that one would expect if the American government was controlled by an oligarchy of wealthy donors whose chief concern is being paid off with tax cuts and deregulation. Put another way, because the congressional Republicans who currently run Congress are effectively controlled by their wealthy donors, the bill reflects the interests of the latter and not the interests of the vast majority of Americans whom Republicans purport to represent.

The tax bill is further evidence of constitutional rot—the gradual descent of republican government into oligarchy. These tendencies have especially affected the Republican Party because it has been the dominant political party during the Reagan regime; although the same forces of oligarchy and concentrated wealth have also constrained—and even crippled—the political imagination and ambitions of the Democrats.

The basic organization of oligarchical politics, with suitable variations for different parts of the country, has been refined over many campaign cycles, and now works something like this: Wealthy donors use gaps and loopholes in the federal campaign finance laws (gaps and loopholes made possible by Republican-appointed judges and a comatose Federal Elections Commission) to give Republican candidates large sums of money (often in secret) to finance their campaigns and purchase campaign ads. The campaign ads often focus on culture-war issues like abortion, religious liberty, gun rights, and immigration; they play upon and stoke cultural and racial resentments, and they assert that Republicans are fighting for the interests of the average person against arrogant secular elites. Then, once in power, Republicans focus on passing regressive tax cuts and deregulation that benefit their wealthy donors, and the latter reward Republicans with further campaign contributions. Rinse and repeat.

Throughout our exchange of letters, I have argued that no matter how dominant the Republican Party may appear at present, it has lost its way and is ripe for a correction. The events of the last nine months merely provide further evidence of this thesis. The party, long since cowed by its wealthy donors, is now in thrall to a cult of personality organized around its deranged leader, who is an ignorant, racist demagogue. The party has given up any serious engagement with policy; it single-mindedly pursues plutocracy disguised by an ugly politics of grievance.

The problem is not that congressional Republicans do not understand the toxic nature of their party's leader. Rather, congressional Republicans are willing to put up with an unstable, ignorant, and delusional president who is dangerously unqualified to hold office because they want absolutely nothing to get in the way of tax cuts for their wealthy donors. Let the heavens fall, let the world be consumed in a radioactive holocaust, the rich must get their tax cuts, the wealthy must become even wealthier.

The constitutional rot is deep and profound.

That Republicans were willing to risk the nation's security in the pursuit of tax cuts for the donor class brings us, at last, to the subject of your most recent letter. That subject is of the greatest importance: the power of the modern presidency, especially in the area of foreign policy. Here you and I largely agree about the need for constitutional reform; and once again, Trump's presidency merely makes salient the problems that have been developing for some time. Because Trump is mercurial, corrupt, and incompetent, people fear that he will use the power of the presidency to cause great harm. Yet if Hillary Clinton had been elected, both of us would still have many of the same concerns about the way presidential power has mutated since World War II.

Throughout our exchanges, I have argued that most of the problems in our democracy can be fixed without a new constitutional convention or an Article V amendment. But in this letter, I will take a different approach. Solving the problem of presidential power requires a serious rethinking of constitutional structure; and I will propose a change—a change that you and I have written about together—that does require an amendment.

Presidential Dictatorship

Seven years ago, in 2010, we wrote that the modern American presidency increasingly has features of a constitutional dictatorship.[1] By "dictatorship," we meant the ability to govern unilaterally or by executive decree. The idea of a *constitutional* dictatorship—that is, one sanctioned by the Constitution—is not new. The Roman Republic employed temporary dictatorships for emergency situations, which were strictly limited in time. During the period of emergency set by the Senate, a Roman dictator could make decisions quickly and unilaterally, and even contrary to established law; upon expiration, the normal legal system was restored.

That is not how the American system of constitutional dictatorship works. Instead, from time to time, the country faces various emergencies, real or imagined. In response, Congress creates statutes—often quite open-ended—that empower the president to exercise discretion in a number of different areas and, perhaps equally important, to make declarations that unlock government capacities and government funding for emergencies. These statutes normally do not sun-

1. Sanford Levinson and Jack M. Balkin, "Constitutional Dictatorship: Its Dangers and Its Design," *Minnesota Law Review* 94 (2010): 1789.

set. Instead, they remain available for future presidents to employ, often assisted by clever executive branch lawyers who figure out how to adapt old grants of power to new situations. During the 2008–2009 financial crisis, for example, government lawyers interpreted statutes empowering the Federal Reserve that were passed during the Hoover administration.

Because of the standard pattern of American state building—the president calls for power to meet emergencies, Congress delegates it, and the president pockets the grant of authority for future occasions— presidents usually have plausible arguments that they act within the law in emergencies rather than having to go outside it. After the 9/11 terrorist attacks, there was a resurgence of interest among academics in Carl Schmitt's theory that the true sovereign is the person who can make exceptions to the legal order. Many academics feared that, for example, President George W. Bush, the self-described "decider," was, or would prove to be, a Schmittian sovereign. But Schmitt's sovereign dictator has never made much sense in the American context. Rather, American presidents are more like what Schmitt would have called "commissarial dictators"—they act according to (plausible) legal authority granted by Congress.

More generally, the modern administrative state allows the president, acting through executive agencies, to fill out the details of general legal standards enacted by Congress in a wide range of areas of domestic policy. But in the area of war and foreign policy, the president's unilateral powers are far greater. The president enjoys wide discretion to direct the conduct of foreign affairs, move troops and resources around the globe, repel threats, and even preemptively use military force—including planes, drones, bombs, and nuclear weapons. The president's power to use force and commit troops is often contested in American politics. Yet, although individual members of Congress often complain about what the president does, Congress as a whole usually does little to stop him.

The American model of presidential dictatorship, unlike the Roman, is not time limited. It occurs during periods of normal politics as well as periods of emergency. It is limited by the scope of previous congressional authorizations, and by congressional decisions to refuse appropriations for particular programs or activities. The president, however, armed with a coterie of very smart lawyers, is often able to find ever new ways to expand his powers to act unilaterally in new areas and on new subjects. President Obama employed the president's power of prosecutorial discretion to carve out exemptions for undocumented aliens; President Trump has used his control over the federal bureaucracy to sabotage the Affordable Care Act. In the American model of presidential dictatorship, the president is therefore hemmed in by (1) his practical ability to direct and control the federal bureaucracy; (2) the nature and scope of congressional authorizations and appropriations; and (3) the extent of the creativity of executive branch lawyers. The president cannot do everything unilaterally, but he can do a great deal more than most people—including the 1787 framers—might have imagined.

As political polarization has crippled Congress, the president has become increasingly emboldened to act unilaterally, safe in the knowledge that a Congress that cannot pass legislation has few ways to stop him. As a result, the major player in checking the modern president is the federal judiciary. State attorneys general and civil society actors brought suits to enjoin President Obama's immigration and environmental programs and President Trump's executive orders on immigration and acceptance of refugees. Liberals who decried judicial restraints on Obama's policies have quickly come to see the virtues of a countervailing branch of government in the era of Trump. That, of course, is the point of a system of checks and balances. The problem we face today, however, is that these checks and balances have become attenuated.

Presidential Dictatorship and War

The more the president acts unilaterally, the more important control of the federal courts becomes. But even the federal courts are unlikely to do much to constrain presidential uses of military force around the globe. There are exceptions, but they are truly exceptional. In 1952, in *Youngstown Sheet & Tube Co. v. Sawyer*,[2] the Court held that President Truman could not seize American steel mills to help win the Korean War. But in *Youngstown*, a majority of the Court believed that the president was trying to use national security as an excuse for getting around the Taft-Hartley labor act and settle a domestic labor dispute in the steel industry. Half a century later, the Court limited President

2. 343 U.S. 579 (1952).

George W. Bush's ability to create his own military commissions; it also held that detainees suspected of terrorism had a right to habeas corpus to contest the legality of their confinement. But the Court did not seriously interfere with the president's terrorism policies, much less with his efforts in the wars in Afghanistan and Iraq. And the D.C. Circuit, to which the Supreme Court handed off the job of articulating its decisions, has largely allowed the president free rein in handling detainees at Guantanamo Bay (and elsewhere). In none of these cases did the Court suggest that it would limit the president's ability to commit troops, engage in hostilities abroad, or even use nuclear weapons. My colleague Bruce Ackerman is currently trying to use the federal courts to challenge the legality of America's interventions in Syria and elsewhere. If he succeeds, it would be a major change in constitutional doctrine; it is more likely that the federal courts will raise any number of procedural and technical obstacles.

As you point out, the president's power to commit troops without a congressional declaration of war is a relatively recent invention — dating to the period following World War II and the creation of the modern national security state. Since President Truman, presidents have often claimed that they could send troops into hostilities without Congress's consent. Following the Vietnam War, Congress passed the War Powers Act over President Nixon's veto, but in practice the WPA has done little to constrain presidential adventurism. Once the president uses American troops to initiate "hostilities," the president has sixty days to request congressional authorization or end the fighting. Presidents have treated this as a blank check for brief (i.e., less than sixty-day) military interventions. In the Libya intervention, President Obama's lawyers simply argued that what the U.S. was doing — supporting NATO allies with air strikes — did not count as "hostilities." Therefore the sixty-day clock never ran out. As technology improves and American forces increasingly rely on automated weaponry and robotics, we can expect that this argument will expand: as long as the enemy is unable to shoot at and kill American (human) troops, there are no "hostilities," no matter how much carnage our airplanes, drones, and robot armies generate.

Despite the almost continual use of our armed forces, Congress has not officially declared war since World War II. Instead, it has employed Authorizations for Use of Military Force (AUMFs). Two such statutes form the official authorization for the continuing War on Terror that the United States began in 2001. The October 16, 2002 AUMF authorized the president to "defend the national security of the United States against the continuing threat posed by Iraq." It gave congressional blessing to the disastrous Iraq War; President Obama later invoked it again to justify the war against ISIS that emerged from that disaster. Perhaps more important, the AUMF of September 18, 2001, enacted shortly after the 9/11 terrorist attacks, authorizes the president "to use all necessary and appropriate force" against anyone the president believes is part of Al Qaeda or affiliated organizations or any successor organization "in order to prevent any future acts of international terrorism against the United States." Perhaps unsurprisingly, Presidents Bush, Obama, and Trump have treated this AUMF as a general permission to expand and extend American military operations wherever they feel it necessary—in Pakistan, Syria, Yemen, Niger, and who knows where else. We are now in the sixteenth year of America's Endless War, with no end in sight, and no indication that Congress is serious about concluding it. Because the president can almost always find (or pretend to find) an apostolic succession of terrorism from Al Qaeda to today's (and tomorrow's) terrorist adversaries, he continues to be clothed with full power to make war around the globe. Prudence, rather than law, is his only impediment, and if the president is incautious or ignorant, prudence may not be enough.

You point out yet another problem—a gradual change in military-civilian relations. Trump has surrounded himself with generals, who now direct American foreign policy. The displacement of civilian with military leadership is a symptom of constitutional rot. It is also a response to the perception of rot. America suffers from an increasing loss of trust in its professional and political classes. Trump surrounds himself with generals because he intuits that whether or not Americans respect their political leaders, they do respect the military, which remains one of the few trusted professional elite organizations in American life. He hopes to leverage this trust for political gain. In so doing, however, Trump exacerbates the very problem of trust that led him to turn to the military in the first place.

When people lose faith in civilian leadership, they give power to the military, hoping that the military will prove a more trustworthy guardian of democracy. No doubt many Americans, including many liberals, are breathing a sigh of relief that Trump is under the adult supervision of disciplined, patriotic military officers. But this attitude represents a dangerous tendency in a republic. So far, our military leaders have behaved professionally, but we cannot assume that this will continue forever. Indeed, the more Americans rely on the military to make up for deficiencies in civilian leadership, the more the military will assume that they have a natural right to lead. This may produce a vicious cycle that destroys the basic constitutional principle of civilian control over the military.

Presidential Dictatorship and the Hard-Wired Constitution

The accumulation of presidential power in domestic policy and war has not come from changes in the hard-wired Constitution. Instead, it has arisen from political practice — aided and abetted by congressional statutes — and from changes in the technology and strategy of warfare. These elements scramble your categories of the Constitution of Settlement and the Constitution of Conversation. On the one hand, these developments are features of the Constitution of Settlement, because they reflect customary practices. Yet they are also part of the Constitution of Conversation, because they are repeatedly (and endlessly) debated by law professors and politicians, and judges.

The current configuration of executive power, unlike the presidential veto or equal representation of states in the Senate, does not flow inexorably from the hard-wired Constitution. And in matters of domestic policy — including the use of the administrative state — presidents are subject to judicial review and to the development of judicial doctrine. So, at least in the domestic arena, some (but not all) constitutional reform of executive power might proceed through legislation and doctrinal development.

But here I will make a Levinsonian point: The root causes of the gradual accumulation of presidential power can be traced in part to features in the hard-wired Constitution. The Constitution's separation of powers, combined with entirely predictable changes in modes of governance (the rise of bureaucracy) and geostrategic considerations (the rise of America as a world power), encourage the executive to aggrandize power over time. Put another way, the very features that Alexander Hamilton saw as the advantages of a unitary executive — energy, initiative, secrecy, and dispatch — combined with the growth of the military and the federal bureaucracy, and the development of political party allegiances, have conspired to make the president much more powerful vis-à-vis Congress, and Congress increasingly inept and impotent in the face of executive overreaching. That the process took two hundred years to complete, a Levinsonian might say, is no reason to doubt that the seeds of the problem already lay in the hard-wired Constitution. It took the development of the administrative state and America's emergence as a global power to activate them. But they have been activated, and the problem is now before us.

In the area of domestic policy, it is plausible to think that at least some constitutional reform could come from judicial development of doctrine and from popular mobilization that leads to congressional legislation limiting the president. Of the two branches, the judiciary may prove to be more important, because even if Congress has the political will to make changes, the president can block reforms with the veto. Matters are different, however, in the area of warfare. Courts play only a minor role in policing presidential power; conversely, one could say that their relative reluctance to exercise judicial review tends to legitimate the growth of presidential power and presidential adventurism.

Your letter also mentions another worrisome tendency—the recent decline in civilian control of the military. And here, I think, a similar analysis applies. On the one hand, this, too, is a result of informal constitutional change. The Constitution makes the president—a civil officer—commander in chief, and it gives Congress the power to regulate the armed forces, but it specifies little else about military-civilian relations. Federal statutes restrict military personnel from serving in certain governmental positions, but Congress has recently made exceptions. One does not need a constitutional amendment to reform the situation: Congress could refuse to make any more exceptions, and it could reinforce the principle of civilian control through new legislation.

On the other hand, one might well argue that our system of separation of powers, while not the sole cause of the decline in civilian control of the military, can make things worse over time. A system of separated powers creates rival power centers; it also may lead to gridlock, exacerbating popular distrust of government. (This is connected to Juan Linz's famous argument about the pathologies of presidential systems.) As trust in government declines, the president and Congress may vie for support of the military, creating a vicious cycle that undermines civilian control.

How the American Constitution Affects the World

One reason why the president's power over foreign affairs matters so much is that the American president is a singularly crucial figure in maintenance of world peace and prosperity. The American system of government helped America grow rich, powerful, and influential—so rich, powerful, and influential that today we are the most important nation on Earth. It follows, therefore, that dysfunction in the American Constitution threatens not only Americans, but everyone else in the world. At this point in history, people all over the world have an interest in a well-functioning American political system, and therefore in a well-functioning American Constitution.

Like many Americans, you worry that Trump will unwisely get us into another war and, even more terrifyingly, provoke an exchange of nuclear weapons. But even if these events never come to pass, Trump remains a singular menace to both American national security and world peace. There is a genuine danger that Trump will severely damage our alliances and our position as the undisputed leader of the liberal international world order.

In a very short space of time, Trump may manage to destroy a carefully constructed legal, political, and economic order, built up through many decades of sacrifice and hard work, that not only serves American interests, but also promotes international law and the use of diplomacy over resort to violence, and has managed to secure peace over most of Europe for several generations. This system is hardly perfect: it favors American and European interests even when they are very unjust, and it has not eliminated violence and abuses of human rights around the world. Nevertheless, it is likely that both the United States and the rest of the world would be much worse off without it.

Trump took power at a crucial moment in world history. China, Russia, India, Iran, and other nations have become stronger and more influential. China would like to displace us as the world's preeminent power; Russia would like to knock us down a peg so that it can rise in comparative status. Interests are shifting, creating the opportunity for new alliances and new priorities. Our most steadfast allies, Europe and Japan, wonder whether they can or should continue to rely on

American leadership. With careful management, the United States might be able to preserve the liberal world order and its preeminent position within that order, just as it did through many previous crises and challenges. But at this crucial moment, Donald Trump, even if he never stumbles into war, has the power to destroy all that Americans have worked for in the last seventy years, undermine America's place in the world, and generate a setback for world peace and prosperity from which we may never recover. If any one person has the power to bring an end to America's leadership and destroy America's power to do good in the world, it is not Xi Jinping or Vladimir Putin—it is Donald Trump.

Impeachment

What, then, are we to do with Trump, who seems more unhinged every day? You despair of using the Constitution's impeachment provisions, at least if we play by existing rules; you also object to Cass Sunstein's lawyerly approach, which refuses to treat Trump as a special case. You and I do agree on one point: impeachment is an inadequate remedy for failed or incompetent presidents, and we should adopt reforms that allow for votes of no confidence, as I describe below.

Before discussing these reforms, however, it is worth noting the pros and cons of impeachment and removal under Article II and removal under the Twenty-Fifth Amendment. Impeachment is hardly a perfect solution to our current problems. Nevertheless, I think it is important to emphasize the advantages of the "lawyerly approach" to impeachment that you criticize.

First, impeachment is a political act, not a legal one. Therefore constitutional grounds for impeachment do not have to conform to the technicalities of American criminal law. The president need not satisfy all of the elements of a recognized criminal offense to commit a "high Crime[] and Misdemeanor[]" under the meaning of Article II. If the president disgraces his office, the House may impeach him. The question of whether such disgrace of office justifies removal is a prudential judgment for the Senate.

In fact, one of the difficulties produced by the Clinton impeachment is that Clinton's defenders were sometimes tempted to argue that Clinton should not be impeached because he did not technically commit a crime, and that the fact that he acted disgracefully should be

irrelevant to Congress's deliberations. In fact, the better argument—
which, thankfully, his defenders also made—was that his conduct,
while thoroughly deserving of censure, was not sufficiently egregious
to require removing him from office. That is a question of prudence,
not of criminal law.

Second, the expression "high Crimes and Misdemeanors," taken
from the English common law, is subject to common law evolution
through practice. Because courts do not regularly construe this part
of the Constitution, the phrase must be defined through political contest. The effective meaning of "high Crimes and Misdemeanors" has
changed over time. The acquittal of Justice Samuel Chase in 1805
shaped the meaning of the phrase, for example, by confirming that
judges could not be removed for purely ideological reasons. The terms
further evolved as a result of the Andrew Johnson and Clinton im-
peachments, and Nixon's resignation under threat of impeachment.

Third, although you worry that lawyers will be hamstrung by legal
niceties and unable to adapt Article II to the extraordinary circumstances of Trump's presidency, you of all people are aware that lawyers are more than able to adapt vague language to untested circumstances. In your 1988 book, *Constitutional Faith*, you point out that
nothing is more characteristic of lawyers than to "beat[] the text into
. . . shape" to meet the necessities of the time.[3] Why should the text
of the impeachment clause be any different? Indeed, the impeachment clause is a perfect example of the Constitution of Conversation,
which, you remind us, requires no constitutional amendment to alter
or reform. Lawyers are perfectly adept at using standards, principles,
and vague terms in arguments that sound lawyerly and principled—
and that purport to apply "neutral principles of constitutional law," in
Herbert Wechsler's famous phrase—but nevertheless get them where
they want to go. If you want a lawyerly brief for removing Trump that
applies to him alone, nothing could be easier.

Even so, the remedy of impeachment has serious defects. Both of
us agree that it is not well designed to deal with the particular problems of the presidency that most concern us. Moreover, impeachment
and removal take months, and in the meantime an unstable president
still controls the armed forces and the nation's nuclear arsenal. As you

3. Sanford Levinson, *Constitutional Faith*, rev. ed. (Princeton University Press,
2011), 177.

recall, following his impeachment, Bill Clinton launched air strikes on Kosovo while the Senate deliberated over whether to remove him.

The Clinton impeachment, however, was exceptional: One of the remarkable features of that period was the ability of both Clinton and the Republican-controlled Congress to compartmentalize. The Senate tried Clinton in the mornings, and then struck deals with him in the afternoon. Trump, by contrast, is not known for his ability to control his emotions. Trump may be unable to do anything other than act from spite or revenge during an impeachment trial. The government will likely shut down far more than during the Clinton impeachment, and it is possible that Trump may send it spiraling into even greater failures. We need a method of removing an incompetent and dangerous leader that quickly resolves the question of succession of power, preserves political stability, and allows the country to move on.

The Twenty-Fifth Amendment

What of the Twenty-Fifth Amendment? Section 4 of the Twenty-Fifth Amendment provides that if the vice president and a majority of the cabinet (or another body that Congress provides) declare "that the President is unable to discharge the powers and duties of his office, the Vice President shall immediately assume the powers and duties of the office as Acting President." However, the president can reject their finding and call for a congressional vote on the question; he regains control unless two-thirds of each house finds against him. (Compare this with impeachment and removal, which requires only a majority of the House and two-thirds of the Senate.)

The Constitution does not define when "the President is unable to discharge the powers and duties of his office." The primary motivation for Section 4 of the Twenty-Fifth Amendment concerns situations in which presidents are physically incapacitated, unconscious, or hovering between life and death, like President James Garfield. In these situations, the vice president and the members of the cabinet have the strongest grounds for intervening. Even then, they may hesitate to displace the president for fear of being accused of staging an illegal coup.

The language of Section 4 seems to cover mental disability, it is true. But it is likely to prove much harder to remove a president who is alert, fully conscious, not physically debilitated, and who asserts that he is just fine, thank you very much—especially if the president continues to enjoy support from his political base. Section 4 of the Twenty-Fifth Amendment is best designed for a President Garfield and not a President Caligula. The Roman emperor Caligula was infamous for his depravity, mania, and cruelty, engaging in increasingly outrageous acts while the Roman nobility cowered before him. Eventually he was assassinated by the Praetorian Guard, suggesting that if there is no easy way to remove an incompetent and deranged ruler, the military may feel forced to take matters into its own hands. Surely there is a better way.

A Congressional Vote of No Confidence

In our article on constitutional dictatorship, we suggested a vote of no confidence for presidents. A vote of no confidence mechanism would allow Congress to remove the president before a scheduled election without also having to prove that the president is disabled or that the president has committed an impeachable offense. There are many ways of organizing such a procedure. For example, it might require supermajorities (of 60 percent or two-thirds) of both houses. It might require that Congress must designate a successor from the president's own party. Or it might require that upon a vote of no confidence, *both* Congress and the president must face new elections so that members of Congress must also put their own jobs on the line and the president is able to make his or her case to the public for reinstatement. Different structures will create slightly different incentives, and so any proposal would require careful study.

As you and I have written, a vote of no confidence mechanism would have many salutary effects, far outstripping any specific legal regulation of the presidency. At a single stroke, it would strengthen Congress's hand in multiple dimensions and would bolster all other legal requirements that restrain executive discretion—whether they be reporting and internal auditing requirements, congressional oversight mechanisms, or judicial review of administrative action. After a vote of no confidence, Congress might impose new restrictions or oversight requirements on the incoming president as a condition of taking office; indeed, the mere fact that his or her predecessor had been removed would serve as a warning of what the next president should and should not do.

In general, the mere possibility of a no confidence motion will make it easier for Congress to pass legislation regulating the president without fear that the president will veto it; it will also make presidents more accountable to Congress and less likely to reject or frustrate oversight mechanisms. At the margins, presidents will be less likely to stiff-arm Congress or veto its laws if they know that Congress can turn around and veto them. Conversely, a no confidence mechanism might also give Congress additional incentives to supervise and take responsibility for a failing presidency, because voters may demand to know why their representatives are allowing an incompetent or corrupt president to stay in office.

Because a vote of no confidence does not require a showing of "high Crimes and Misdemeanors," much less a full-blown trial in the Senate, it changes the calculations of what is politically thinkable for Congress to do. Representatives and senators may well hesitate at committing themselves to an impeachment trial, which will hijack legislative agendas for months; by contrast, a vote of no confidence can be scheduled quickly and a new leader sworn in immediately.

Finally, although a no confidence mechanism would not by itself cure political polarization, it might tend to produce presidents who are closer to the median member of Congress and thus encourage deal making and agreements across party lines. All of this reflects a general point about structural remedies: because they change incentives generally, they often have multiple substantive effects.

A vote of no confidence does not, however, solve all problems, and ideally we should combine it with reforms to our system of campaign finance (so that the president is not even more at the mercy of the wealthy donor class who presently control Congress) and the elimination of single-member congressional districts (in order to change electoral incentives and partly reduce polarization). These examples suggest why it is important to think about the connections between many different kinds of constitutional reform.

Unlike many of the political reforms I've discussed in our exchanges, this one *does* require a constitutional amendment. Sadly, I suspect that such an amendment will only come after the United States has suffered a catastrophe or something perilously close to it. If no amendment is forthcoming, Congress may have to settle on a new interpretation of "high Crimes and Misdemeanors," thus changing the effective requirements for impeachment and removal. But there is no guarantee that this single interpretive change will produce all of the same beneficial effects as a well-thought-out structural amendment.

I am therefore delighted to close this letter to you on a note of agreement with your central thesis. Here, I believe, is an example of an important and beneficial political reform that really does require Article V.

Jack

PART SIX

CONCLUSIONS

JANUARY 1, 2018

Dear Jack,

The beginning of 2018—which we all hope will be better than the dreadful past year—serves as the more or less arbitrary close of our "epistolary exchanges" that began over two years ago when the world was very, very different. Any cessation of our exchanges would be arbitrary, because quite obviously future possibilities—some of which will be known to our readers in a way that they could not possibly be truly known (or perhaps even confidently predicted) by us—will affect the validity of our necessarily tentative analyses. My task in this final missive is to offer some conclusions as to what I have learned, even as I have come to appreciate more than ever the truth of Yogi Berra's caution that "it's tough to make predictions, especially about the future."

Though we took Donald Trump seriously enough to include him in our early analyses, it's safe to say that both of us were astounded by his attaining the Oval Office, as were, of course, almost all "professional predictors." The *New York Times*'s "prediction meter" indicated that Hillary Clinton had an 85 percent probability of winning; even the more cautious Nate Silver viewed her as a 69 percent favorite. I suspect that the meter might itself have affected the vote in Wisconsin and Michigan, where supporters of Jill Stein might have thought there was no potential cost in casting a protest vote instead of voting for one (presumably Clinton) of the presumptively flawed candidates. Trump's margin was less than Stein's vote in Wisconsin and Michigan. Had Clinton carried both states, the final electoral vote would have been tied at 270 apiece. If one adds Pennsylvania to the mix, then it's possible that enough additional Clinton voters would have taken the trouble to vote had they really believed that Donald Trump might become the next president. Obviously, we'll never know. We know only what did in fact happen, and our letters back and forth in the past year since November 9 have represented our best efforts to make sense of our current situation, even if the outlook appears quite grim. But I continue to remind friends every time I have the chance that the outlook would have appeared to be grim even had Clinton won.

So let me proceed simply by listing four primary takeaways that, I hope, transcend simply commentary on current events. In the past month alone, for example, we've had both the remarkable election of Doug Jones in Alabama and the passage of the tax bill rammed through Congress by a militant Republican majority unconcerned with any plausible notion of what might be termed "legislative due process." I shall return to this latter point anon. But I want to begin by what I think are the two most important generalizations that, for better or worse, might remain relevant to our readers even several years from now:

1. Presidential Dictatorship

For all of the emphasis in our standard descriptions of the American political system of "separation of powers," we do live, in a non-trivial sense, under presidential dictatorship.

This is not a new insight. One of our many collaborations now almost a decade ago pointed to the prescience of Clinton Rossiter's troubling 1948 book *Constitutional Dictatorship* and its emphasis on the degree to which even the United States could at certain points in its past, and even more likely in its post–World War II (and nuclear) future, be described in such terms. What this means is not simply the ever-increasing role of the state per se, which was accurately predicted by opponents of the U.S. Constitution in 1787–88 (who condemned "consolidated government") and ably defended by Publius in *The Federalist*, who insisted that the scope of governmental power needed to be commensurate with the challenges facing the new and vulnerable country. Rather, what Rossiter focused on, and what has become perhaps the single most pressing issue of our current time, is the aggrandizement of executive power. For a variety of reasons, some of which will be addressed below, legislatures appear to have weakened decision-making authority around the world, and strong executives are stepping up to make what are viewed as necessary decisions. I have for several years now emphasized the relevance of Carl Schmitt, who wrote in 1923 (and then a second edition in 1926) *The Crisis of Parliamentary Democracy*, which incisively analyzed the failures of the Weimar Parliament to serve as a genuinely legitimate deliberator and then legislator about the challenges that faced postwar German society. But decisions did have to be made, and increasingly they would be made by strong executives, including German chancellors who could invoke the notorious Article 48 of the Weimar Constitution to exercise "emergency powers." Not surprisingly, Schmitt also wrote a notable book on dictatorship that provided some of the basis for his support of Hitler in the mid-1930s. He was a dreadful man who, alas, saw deeply into some of the problems of contemporary politics.

It is an embarrassing truth that both partisan Democrats and Republicans have been more than happy to defend executive aggrandizement so long as it is their president who is pushing various envelopes of traditional understandings of executive authority. "Whataboutism" has become a term of rhetorical art in the current era, signifying the propensity of Republicans, when asked about overreaching by George W. Bush or Donald Trump, to say, "What about Barack Obama's remarkable expansion of drone strikes, in some cases against American citizens in countries with which we formally were not at war or his unilateral decision regarding DACA, 'Deferred Action for Child Arrivals,' i.e., children brought by their parents to the United States whose legal authority to remain in the United States is highly contestable?" In turn, Democrats accuse Republicans of selective outrage by asking, "What about George W. Bush's embrace, during his first term, of torture and other 'enhanced' means of interrogation in violation of both U.S. and international law or Donald Trump's arbitrary attempts to rewrite American immigration policy on the basis of anti-Muslim bigotry?"

The blunt fact is that there is no truly satisfying theory, constitutional or otherwise, of contemporary executive power. There are some truly excellent books, like that of Stephen Griffin, explaining the inexorable rise of presidential power in the aftermath of World War II. A key figure, of course, was the modest man from your home state of Missouri, Harry Truman, who both unilaterally entered the Korean War in June 1950 and then, almost a year later, attempted to seize the

American steel industry in order to assure the production of adequate war matériel in the face of a threatened strike by unionized steelworkers. He was, of course, rebuffed by the Supreme Court (over an eloquent dissent by Chief Justice Fred Vinson, joined by two colleagues), but it may be relevant that not only did Truman's action push the envelope of executive power but also that he enjoyed only a 22 percent approval rating among the public at the time. The Court really took no risk in invalidating the seizure (unless it had turned out, counterfactually, that Truman was in fact right that the strike that followed the Supreme Court's decision would in fact harm the U.S. war effort).

Truman was succeeded in office by Dwight Eisenhower, who in fact seemed to have a more restrained view of his power as president. Quite notably, he explained to Anthony Eden that he could not on his own join England, France, and Israel in their ill-fated attempt to regain the Suez Canal by attacking Egypt in 1956 because Congress would have to authorize it, and Ike saw no reason to believe they would (or, for that matter, should). But then, of course, Eisenhower was succeeded in turn by the charismatic John F. Kennedy, who promised to "get America moving again" after the ostensibly soporific years of the Eisenhower presidency. My own view, which I've articulated in an earlier letter, is that a truly fateful episode in our history was the Cuban Missile Crisis of 1962, in which Kennedy not only took the world to the brink of thermonuclear war without any serious consultation with Congress, but also gained apparently undying support among the American people, who seem still in the grip of Camelot. What Kennedy did was to establish a template for presidential vigor—or perhaps one should say "energy," one of the favorite terms of Publius in *The Federalist* when defending the need for a strong president.

It now seems widely agreed—at least among members of the general public and even, I am sad to say, among many of our professional legal academic colleagues—that the presidential commander-in-chief power includes unilateral authority to deploy American armed forces anywhere in the world, at any time, against any presidentially deemed foe. Everyone knows that the last declarations of war by Congress occurred with regard to World War II, and everyone knows as well that that was scarcely the last major, let alone "minor," war that the United States has engaged in over the past seventy-five years. To be sure, beginning with the disastrous Gulf of Tonkin Resolution, Congress has seemingly been more than willing to delegate vast powers to the president. (Perhaps one should revive Justice Benjamin Cardozo's imprecations against "delegation run riot" in one of the New Deal cases that attempted, altogether unsuccessfully, to supply limits to Congress's ability to delegate power to the president.) America's current wars, the longest in our history, are being carried on under the ostensible terms of the Authorization for Use of Military Force (AUMF) in 2001 and 2002 following the September 11 attacks and the subsequent desire to invade Iraq and destroy Saddam Hussein's regime in that country.

There are a few notable members of Congress, both Democratic and Republican, who have protested against reliance on what is clearly an outmoded AUMF, but they have gotten nowhere with their colleagues. After all, to engage in a serious debate about presidential authority and American adventurism abroad would require that members of Congress actually exercise some public (and necessarily accountable) responsibility with regard to the use of force (and the killing of both Americans and foreigners), which they seem entirely unwilling to do. The truly terrible possibility of a catastrophic war in the Korean peninsula seems to have become accepted; all too few are willing to support legislation clearly establishing that the president has no authority to wage war, especially where the use of nuclear weapons might be involved either offensively or defensively by the country being attacked by the U.S., without explicit authority of Congress, unless we are the victims of unequivocal attack by another country.

Perhaps the most truly dismaying sentence I've read in the past year appeared in the *Washington Post* on November 14, 2017: "Senators trying to prevent President Trump from launching an unprovoked nuclear attack were stymied Tuesday, after a panel of experts warned them against rewriting laws to restrain a commander in chief many worry is impulsive and unpredictable enough to start a devastating international crisis." These "experts" were bipartisan. Thus Brian McKeon, who served in the Defense Department during the Obama administration, declared, "If we were to change the decision-making process because of a distrust of this president, that would be an unfortunate decision for the next president." I confess I read this as a concession that we live under a presidential dictatorship even (or especially) on such monumental matters, and that we should be wary of limiting the power of the next person we elect as our dictator.

C. Wright Mills, an important radical critic writing in the 1950s and '60s, coined the term "crackpot realism" to refer to widely accepted

predicates of the American social and political process during that
era. I confess that I find McKeon to exemplify such "crackpot realism"
in our own time. Were it John Yoo (who authored the infamous "torture memo" in 2002, about which we earlier wrote) who proclaimed
the necessity of submitting to Donald Trump's de facto unilateral authority, one would expect political liberals to scream, as was in fact the
case when the memo was revealed in 2004. But Yoo's embrace of what
he termed the "Hanoverian presidency," modeled after the powers
of the British monarch in the eighteenth century, has seemingly become near-conventional wisdom. (And, in fairness to Yoo, one should
note that he has written several eloquent columns attacking Trump's
overreaching.) As I learned during a remarkable conversation among
many members of the Harvard Law School faculty this past fall, it is
now regarded as basically naïve to suggest that there are constitutional
limits (especially if one might even suggest they are enforceable by the
judiciary) on the ability of presidents to act in the realms of foreign
and military policy. There may be, as Yoo himself insisted, theoreti-
cal political limits; he noted, for example, that Congress retained the
power of the purse and could simply refuse to fund presidential programs. But no one should take practical solace in this possibility. Recall that even Abraham Lincoln, who believed that the Mexican War
was unconstitutional, nonetheless voted, in his one term as congress-
man, to support the troops by providing them necessary supplies.

One of Rossiter's principal points, which I agree with more than
ever, is that the United States has a particularly dangerous form of constitutional dictatorship, for several reasons. One of them, even if not
the most important, perhaps, is the fact that the United States Constitution combines the roles of head of state with head of government.
The American president, regardless of political party, is accorded a
status far more befitting a monarch than a head of a purported "Republican Form of Government." Ross Perot, when he was running for
the presidency in 1992, emphasized that we should consider the president to be a mere "employee," capable of being assessed ruthlessly by
his (or her) employer, the American people.

But it is also worth emphasizing that the basis on which we select
our presidents rarely includes paying much attention to their actual
levels of knowledge or demonstrated capacity for prudent judgment
with regard to delicate issues of foreign and military policy. No president since George H. W. Bush could be said to be seriously qualified in

that respect. I in fact supported Barack Obama in 2008 because I had more faith in his judgment—he had, after all, opposed the Iraq War while Hillary Clinton had authorized the delegation of authority to initiate such a war to George W. Bush—but it would be almost absurd to claim that Obama had the level of experience we might want in a commander in chief, which was true as well, of course, of both his predecessor and, most spectacularly, of his successor. "We the People" seem to be like parents willing to give their six-year-old a book of easily lit matches and then going out for dinner, hoping that nothing amiss happens in our absence.

2. Structures Matter

Structures count, and Americans are almost pathologically averse to discussing the potential problems with our national constitutional framework.

You will surely not be surprised by this second takeaway. I'm afraid that I've become a crank about both the relevance of the structures established by the 1787 Constitution and, perhaps more importantly, the extent to which they have generated near-pathological dysfunctionalities that threaten the maintenance of our republic (and, beyond that, perhaps our very lives). The easiest example, of course, is the Electoral College, which is the sole explanation for the fact that Donald Trump and not Hillary Clinton is our president today. Everyone knows that Clinton visited Florida twenty-five times and Wisconsin not at all following the Wisconsin primary in the spring of 2016. That is legitimately taken as a sign of the stupidity of her campaign strategy. But no one criticizes her for failing to campaign vigorously in California, Texas, New York, or Massachusetts, because, unlike Wisconsin, no one ever thought that those states were "in play." As a matter of fact, Clinton did considerably better in Texas than most recent Democratic nominees, but almost no one took account of that fact, as Texas continued to go predictably Republican (and California, New York, and Massachusetts predictably Democratic). No sane constitutional drafters would today construct the Electoral College as a mechanism for presidential selection; majorities of Americans polled since 1944 have agreed that the Electoral College should be abolished in favor of direct election. But, of course, nothing has (or, almost certainly, will) be done, because of another dreadful feature of the Constitution: Article V, which, as practical matter, makes it nearly impossible to amend the Constitution with regard to anything truly significant. The last such amendment was the Twenty-Second Amendment, ratified in 1951, limiting presidents to serving two terms in office. One can view that as Republican revenge on Franklin Roosevelt or as a decision by the American people that he had in fact violated our "unwritten Constitution" by breaking the two-term tradition established by the great George Washington, who could surely have served as president for life. Instead, in the great words of Lin-Manuel Miranda, he taught the American people "how to say goodbye" instead of submitting to the cult of the indispensable great man/leader. (Nelson Mandela in the twentieth century provided another such rare example, as against all too many presidents, throughout the world, who repeatedly ran for reelection or fought to amend constitutions that imposed term limits.)

But the Electoral College and Article V are relatively low-hanging fruit. The former has been the subject of over six hundred proposed amendments to change or abolish it, albeit unsuccessful, while the latter has, in the views of some of our colleagues, including the aforementioned Bruce Ackerman, been at least somewhat tamed through the mechanism of de facto amendment "outside" of Article V. The New Deal, for Ackerman, is the most notable instance, though one might easily regard the development of the near-omnipotent warrior president following World War II, as set out, and basically defended, by Griffin, as at least an equally important de facto revision of our prior constitutional order.

But our entire institutional structure needs at least rethinking, even if not, perhaps, replacement. The most important lesson taught to us by the framers was the one spelled out by Publius in *Federalist* No. 1 that "We the People" were capable of genuine "reflection and choice" as to how we wished to be governed. I fear that almost no one truly believes this any longer, especially, I must say, within the legal academy. The primary motif instead seems to be a genuine fear of popular judgment (a view amply reinforced, needless to say, by the disaster of the 2016 national election). But the alternative to such reflection and choice is to be mired in the consequences of what political scientists call "path dependence," that is, the choices made by earlier generations that now seem insurmountable.

Consider (briefly) the United States Congress, both the House and the Senate. Should anyone have genuine faith in the legitimacy of these venerable bodies? The House is distorted by the consequences of ever-more-ruthless partisan gerrymandering and the distortions produced by the congressional requirement of single-member districts. As to the former, one can argue that it is unconstitutional, a premise that the Supreme Court will consider in what is almost certain to be its most important single decision in 2018. [As a matter of fact, the Court punted the issue.] As to single-member districts, the Constitution is silent, inasmuch as they are the result of congressional legislation in 1842, readopted by Congress in 1967.

Path dependence is an extremely powerful force, and we are imprisoned within one of the worst electoral systems in the world. The fact that we could "reform" the House by the "mere" passage of legislation—that is, a requirement, for example, that all states with delegations larger than six representatives adopt multi-member districts whose winners would be chosen through a process of proportional voting—is, politically, a fantasy. Representatives who have benefited amply by the status quo are completely unlikely to vote for a new system that would be extremely destabilizing and would cost many of them their seats. This is in fact one of the reasons I continue to support a new constitutional convention, because only such a convention, in the hands of a representative sample of "We the People" and not the current elected beneficiaries of an indefensible system, could achieve meaningful reform.

But the House, for all of its problems, is a paragon of democratic legitimacy when compared to the Senate, where the principle of equal representation of the states reigns supreme. The fact that fifty-one Republican senators voted for the December 2017 tax bill, as against the forty-eight Democrats who voted against, cannot even be described accurately as genuine "tyranny of the majority" because the Republicans in fact come from states whose overall population is well short of a majority of the American public. Most dramatically, of course, the two Democratic senators from California, with a current population of approximately 39.5 million persons, were exactly balanced by the two Republicans from Wyoming, with approximately 550,000 persons. To be sure, Vermont's two liberal senators (Bernie Sanders has gone back to describing himself as an independent rather than a Democrat), representing approximately 650,000 residents, canceled out the two votes of Texas's Ted Cruz and John Cornyn and their roughly 28 million constituents. But if one adds up all of the states, one discovers that the forty-eight Democrats represented approximately 54 percent of the national population. Indeed, no poll ever purported to demonstrate that more than roughly one-third of the respondents supported the tax bill.

What is distinctive about this tax bill is not only its provisions that line the pockets of favored special interests. One might well describe this as the American way. My wife, Cynthia, and I, in our book *Fault Lines in the Constitution,* ostensibly written for teenagers, note that both Democratic and Republican senators from the corn-growing states in the upper Midwest are eager to preserve corn subsidies for their constituents, just as Senators Leahy and Sanders no doubt look out for the dairy farmers in Vermont. For better or worse, that's ordinary politics, though what's repulsive about the Senate is that senators from small states (like Vermont) are given far more power than are their colleagues from the large states. Perhaps the most shocking (to readers) visual in our book is one pointing out that less than a majority of the country now live in a total of forty-one states, which receive eighty-two votes in the Senate, while most people in the United States now live in only nine states, with eighteen senators. And by all indications, these disproportions will only get worse in the future. One sometimes hears it said that the small state/large state divide in the Senate is relatively unimportant. That is, alas, nonsense, a bit of comforting ideology that serves to reinforce the legitimacy of an ever more indefensible institution.

But the tax bill cannot be explained only by a desire to help one's local constituents. The decision to cap deductions for state property tax and income tax was motivated by an abject desire to attack the large states—including California, New York, Illinois, and Massachusetts—which are viewed as morally profligate in their willingness to tax their citizenry and spend attendant revenues on such shocking programs as medical care, education, infrastructure, or cultural institutions. They are the beast that must be starved, according to the catechism of anti-tax fanatics like Grover Norquist. Have no doubt: The tax bill is not only class warfare, which it most certainly is, designed to bolster the income and retained wealth of the already extremely rich; it is also an escalation of the culture wars within the United States between right-wing libertarians and culturally conservative Evangelicals, on the one hand, and more communitarian and cosmopolitan progressives who have emigrated from the provinces to urban centers. One might think that the New Yorker Donald Trump might have some solicitude for his home state, but there is no evidence that he truly appreciates what makes New York City so truly special.

One should also address the culture-war aspects of a relatively minor feature of the bill that taxes the investment income of those universities with more than $500 million endowments. Obviously, there are not many, but just as obviously they include America's great research universities. Even N. Gregory Mankiw, the former chief economic advisor to President George W. Bush, notes that there is no economic rationale for this provision that would, for example, force Princeton University to pay taxes equal to roughly $4,000 per individual Princeton student, who are admitted these days on a completely need-blind basis and where every student from a family making less than $65,000 a year receives aid covering all tuition, room, and board. Mankiw describes the universities selected out as "engines of economic growth and opportunity for the middle class," which makes it all the more telling that they are among the victims of the tax bill. "I have yet," he wrote in the *New York Times*, "to see . . . a principled defense of the policy." So what explains it? The answer, he suggests, almost certainly correctly, is the ever more "tribal" nature of American politics. The "deplorables"—Hillary Clinton surely should not have used that term in public, but she was completely correct about many members of Trump's base—who increasingly control the Republican Party wish to humiliate and weaken the Ivy League institutions they view as simple bastions of liberalism (though the conservative Mankiw himself is at Harvard). Perhaps there is a genuine argument to be had about the degree to which aspects of the tax bill are in fact "pro-growth." But there is no genuine argument to make that capping tax deductions in California and New York, or taxing Harvard, Yale, Princeton, or MIT, will enhance American growth or "make America great again."

The cap on the deductibility of state taxes, coupled with the decision to tax America's most important universities that just happen to be located in a small number of blue states, is raw sectional warfare, enabled by what James Madison consistently denounced as the "evil" decision made in 1787 to submit to Delaware's extortionate demand for equal representation in the Senate. Madison accepted what is sometimes valorized as the "great compromise," just as other framers engaged in similar compromises with slave owners by agreeing to en-

hance the representation of slave states in the House of Representatives (and therefore also the Electoral College) by counting their
slaves, albeit as three-fifths of free persons, as part of the basis of representation. In both cases, the rationale was that what the Israeli phi-
losopher Avishai Margalit calls "rotten compromises" were necessary
to attain the overriding end of reaching agreement on a new constitution to replace the "imbecilic" Articles of Confederation. Perhaps that
was true in 1787, but we live with the terrible consequences of those
decisions even today, without adequate justification.

As always, the key question is what is to be done? The Constitution
makes it impossible, practically speaking to "reform" the Senate; every
state must agree to break the rule of equal voting power, and, as with
reforming the electoral system for the House, it is literally fantastic to
imagine that that state of affairs will ever obtain. There are also imagi-
native proposals like those of our friend and colleague Akhil Amar, by
which the Senate would be retained in all of its formal constitutional
glory, save that it would be limited, say, to confirming foreign ambassadors. If one believes that bicameralism is beneficial, as I in fact do,
then one could establish a brand-new "Shmenate," whose members
would be selected on a far more legitimate basis than the current Senate. It could be given jurisdiction over everything now in the purview
of the Senate, save for confirmation of ambassadors. But, obviously,
this is also a mere fantasy.

[On January 16, 2018, shortly after this letter was written, Harvard's
Steven Levitsky and Daniel Ziblatt published *How Democracies Die*,
which stirred wide discussion and became a best-seller. In a review
in the Summer 2018 issue of the journal *Democracy*, I shared much
of the admiration for the book, which shows how Donald Trump dis-
plays many of the pathologies of leaders in a variety of Latin American
and European countries who led their countries toward much more
authoritarian political systems. However, I think the book falls way
short in confronting the possibility that the deficiencies of the formal
constitutional system in the United States might themselves contrib-
ute to the rise of Trumpismo. Like many other critics of the contemporary American political system and its "dysfunctionalities," Levitsky
and Ziblatt have almost literally nothing useful to say about the actual
strengths and weaknesses of the Constitution as a framework of government.

The late Juan Linz, for example, argued that presidential systems were more likely to lead to authoritarianism because they often resulted in gridlock and appeals to the military to resolve them. Although some political scientists have questioned the connection to military coups, there can be little doubt that presidential systems, which by definition create a chief executive who is fundamentally independent of the legislature, accentuate the possibility for what might be described as charismatic Caesarism, where a president claims a mandate to act in behalf of "the people" who placed him in office. This tendency in American politics goes back at least to Andrew Jackson, but it has become much accentuated in an age of mass media, coupled with the loss of faith in legislative institutions. These dangers are, if not absent, then at least significantly mitigated in parliamentary systems that allow a dissatisfied parliamentary majority to "fire" a prime minister through a vote of no confidence. Levitsky and Ziblatt are basically silent on this point and on other important aspects of the formal American system. They spend almost no time discussing constitutional design. Yet it is impossible to discuss "how democracies die" without asking whether constitutional design plays a role. Sooner or later, we will have to discuss the American Constitution in a spirit other than reverential devotion.]

3. "Constitutional Rot" and Constitutional Crisis

You have recently introduced into the conversation, with both this book and in earlier postings on *Balkinization,* the valuable notion of "constitutional rot." You are referring, I believe, to the stench of an increasingly corrupt political order presided over—one dare not say truly "led"—by radically anti-Publian officials who are fully in thrall to the ruling plutocracy. The very best illustration of such rot is the recent tax bill, which is little more than piggery by plutocrats able to manipulate the Republicans who are dependent on their donations in order to finance their campaigns. As our friend Larry Lessig has demonstrated, many of the Republican legislators, like the egregious Speaker of the House Paul Ryan, are sincere believers in plutocratic ideology who don't need to be bribed so much as supported by a donor base sufficient to discourage any realistic competition within the political process. The "donor primary," with some rare exceptions, is at least as, and perhaps more, important than the actual voting primary.

I do think it is important to distinguish "constitutional rot" from

our paradigm of constitutional "crises," whether the events surrounding secession in 1861 or the New Deal. Those "crises" require a self-
conscious decision either to violate the law in order to achieve a higher
objective or an equally self-conscious decision to remain faithful to
legal requirements even when the consequences of doing so appear
disastrous. We also talk about crises of "performance," manifested by
rioting or other forceful demonstrations in the streets and violations
of the "domestic Tranquility" that the Preamble announces as one of
the aims of the Constitution. But I increasingly believe that you may
be underestimating the degree to which pervasive constitutional rot
is itself indicative of the most important kind of "legitimacy crisis."
If one begins looking at purported leaders as "rotten" in fundamental
respects, doesn't this provide the basis for the withdrawal of any kind
of true commitment to the surrounding political system? One might
interpret the years of the American Revolution—or what I increasingly insist on calling the "Secession from the British Empire"—as a
constitutional crisis generated by the conflict over the formal powers
of Parliament especially to tax the British subjects living in the American colonies. There is much to be said for that view. But surely as important was the ideology so classically delineated fifty years ago by
Bernard Bailyn in which proponents of classical republicanism identifying with the "countryside" witheringly criticized the "corruption"
they found almost constitutive of the "court-" (i.e., monarchy-) cen-
tered views of apologists for the British rulers.

So consider the tax bill from a "constitutional rot" perspective. My
major point is not simply to castigate the policies adopted by the Republican Congress and eagerly signed by the plutocrat in chief. Rather,
it is to note the almost literally unprecedented lack of any acceptable
process—what John McCain had earlier described as "order"—in the
writing of the bill. No hearings were held, and such debate as in fact
occurred featured the presentation of knowing lies to the American
public. Given my own obsession, which you are well aware of, with
Justice John Marshall's paradigmatic opinion in *McCulloch v. Maryland*, I could not help but think of the degree to which the process of
the tax bill is, by any measure, the antithesis of the process, at least as
described by Marshall, that gave us the Bank of the United States in
1791. It was one of the most divisive issues of the young republic (and
the trigger for Madison's joining in the formation, with Thomas Jefferson, of the Democratic-Republican Party to contend with Hamilton's

Federalist Party). But consider Marshall's description of the background of the bill incorporating the bank:

> The power now contested was exercised by the first Congress elected under the present constitution. The bill for incorporating the bank of the United States did not steal upon an unsuspecting legislature, and passed unobserved. Its principle was completely understood, and was opposed with equal zeal and ability. After being resisted, first in the fair and open field of debate, and afterwards in the executive cabinet, with as much persevering talent as any measure has ever experienced, and being supported by arguments which convinced minds as pure and as intelligent as this country can boast, it became a law.

Whether or not this process was fully relevant to his decision as to the constitutionality of the bank, it is nonetheless telling that he chose to begin by emphasizing the degree to which the legislation conformed to what we might truly identify with "republican government" at its very best. That is, proponents of the bank, like Hamilton, offered extensive arguments that could in fact be tested in "the fair and open field of debate." One might oppose the bank, as Madison and Jefferson did, but what they could not say is that it sneaked through an "unsuspecting legislature." Note as well the reference to the "pure" and "intelligent" minds who had to be persuaded that Hamilton's arguments were in fact stronger than those proffered by Madison and other opponents of the bank.

Even if one adopts a properly skeptical view of the politics of the early republic, it is still hard to escape the feeling that there were giants in those days who were truly motivated by what we have called in other of our writings "high politics." That is, unlike "low politics" motivated by sheer self-seeking (or what economists call "rent seeking," the capture of public power to line one's pockets) or the crass interests of one's political party and, especially, its donor base, "high politics" involves a genuine good-faith debate about different visions for the country. Perhaps the most remarkable achievement of Lin-Manuel Miranda with regard to his vision of Hamilton is his making plausible the notion that Hamilton was indeed a person of great honor who adopted his views in the genuine belief that they would be good for a country he genuinely loved. And Hamilton proved his honor by

endorsing Jefferson over Burr, not because he had converted in any
way to Jefferson's view, but because he recognized that Jefferson, too,
was a thoughtful patriot, unlike the "voluptuous" and characterologi-
cally corrupt Aaron Burr. And, of course, the Bank Bill was signed
by George Washington after full consultation with all members of his
cabinet, two of whom (Jefferson and Attorney General Edmund Ran-
dolph) suggested that it was unconstitutional, while Hamilton, as one
might expect, vigorously defended it. Even if Washington was not the
true "demigod" that some believed him to be, there can be little doubt
that he patterned himself after the model of Roman virtue and was not
concerned by what would lower his tax liability.

If *McCulloch* sets out a perhaps idealized model of republican government at its very best, then the tax bill is its absolute antithesis.
And this is an issue of true constitutional import. The most basic issue
facing any pluralistic social order like our own is that of legitimacy:
Why exactly should political losers accept their fate? Winners scarcely
have to be convinced of the merits of a political system that rewards
them. It is those who draw the short end of the stick who need reassurance that they were in fact treated fairly, that, in a deep sense, they received "due process of law" before being negatively affected. But there
is no legitimacy to the tax bill. All one can say about it is that it got a
majority of votes in the House and the Senate and was signed by the
most mendacious president in our 230-year history. The tax bill fails on
grounds of both process and substance. And that failure may be evidence of a genuine constitutional illness (or "crisis") that will test the
capacity of the existing political order to govern legitimately.

4. Political Culture Does Matter: On "Diversity" and the Prospects of Secession

So one of my takeaways from this two-year immersion in coming to
terms with Donald Trump and Trumpismo is that political culture does
matter. Although I continue to insist that we in the legal academy—
and the outside punditry and, ultimately, candidates for political
office—should pay more attention to the importance of formal structures, I hope it is clear that I concede that one can scarcely ignore the
importance of what Gabriel Almond and Sidney Verba many years ago
called "the civic culture." It is a technocratic fantasy to believe that a
"well-designed constitution" can save a polity with a political culture

that does not, for example, recognize the existence of plural views and values and the concomitant need to negotiate with adversaries and even make compromises with them for the sake of civic peace. Similarly, it may be the case that there are halcyon polities that could operate effectively—and even justly—under any conceivable set of constitutional structures.

But perhaps the most important question facing not only the United States, but also a multitude of countries throughout the world, is the degree to which a successful polity requires practical limits on the degree of ideological pluralism that can be tolerated. Much is made of the fact that the United States is today more sharply polarized than at any time since the run-up to the Civil War (or War Between the States). "Reconstruction" was ultimately limited by the willingness to pay the price of continued injustice to the enslaved persons (and their descendants), who had ostensibly been freed by the war and the Thirteenth Amendment (which became a practical nullity in terms of what the late Robert Cover labeled its potential "jurisgenerativity"). Whether "Black Lives (Really) Matter" remains an issue in 2018.

A fascinating year-end poll by the *Washington Post* indicates that while 68 percent of all Americans agree that 2017 was good for them personally, at the same time 58 percent believe it has been a bad year for the United States overall. Eighty-one percent express their discontent with the American political system, while 82 percent believe that race relations are worsening. Only 29 percent believe the country is going in the right direction; even 41 percent of Republicans polled apparently believe the country is going in the wrong direction, as do a stunning 94 percent of Democrats. Among those describing themselves as independents, only 27 percent believe the country is going in the right direction. The top twenty words offered by respondents to describe the past year include "chaotic," "crazy," "turbulent," "horrible," and "disastrous," though, to be sure, there were some who described it as "great" and, more neutrally, "eventful" and "intriguing," which presumably all of us can agree with.

American progressives have fully embraced the importance of "diversity" and "multiculturalism." I much prefer, as an individual, living within such social realities. But as a political scientist, I find myself wondering if the American political system—or any national political system?—is really equipped to handle the degree of diversity and multiplicity that we see every day. The most attractive versions of

American political thought—and of constitutional interpretation—emphasize the maximal inclusivity embraced by the term "American" and, therefore, "We the People." Those versions tend toward a universalism that ultimately renders near irrelevant the psychological reality of national borders and polities predicated on preserving any kind of "national" identities or cultures.

From this perspective, "patriotism" is surely the last refuge of scoundrels; instead we should pledge our loyalty to a nascent world community in which all of us are truly the recipients of equal concern and respect. But a grim truth of our present world is that relatively few people seem really eager to follow Martha Nussbaum's imprecations to become truly cosmopolitan in our identifications and loyalties. Even if the worst forms of organic nationalism seem to have been at least somewhat beaten back in many countries around the world, it is hard to gainsay the increased identity politics more generally—and the conflicts that identity politics predictably generate. As Justice Holmes said, "we live by symbols," and public confrontation over their display, as in public monuments or willingness to "honor" the flag and the national anthem.

More ominously, perhaps, we must recognize the degree, as Rogers Smith pointed out some years ago, that American political thought is characterized not only by what to us is an attractive liberal universalism, but also by a distinctly less attractive note of ascriptivism. As you know, I have in some of my recent writings emphasized the importance of *Federalist* No. 2, not because I agree with it, but because I think it captures a reality of our constitutional tradition that we prefer to ignore even as it helps to explain, in its own way, the awfulness of our recent politics (including, for that matter, Charlottesville and the manifestation of an open renewal of "white supremacy" as a political value). Publius—in actuality the New Yorker John Jay—wrote, "Providence has been pleased to give this one connected country to one united people—a people descended from the same ancestors, speaking the same language, professing the same religion, attached to the same principles of government, very similar in their manners and customs. . . ." This was preposterous even in 1787 when he wrote it; after all, the Constitution was translated from English to German and Dutch shortly after its public release in September 1787 so that German speakers in Pennsylvania and Dutch speakers in New York could understand what the framers were proposing. It is far more preposterous today, when, to take only two examples drawn from religion, there are more Buddhists than Presbyterians in Houston, Texas, and one of the most important American religions is the Mormon Church, created only in the 1830s by the religious entrepreneurship of the prophet Joseph Smith.

What we have to ask, though, is not whether Jay is a reliable sociological guide, where the answer is surely not. Rather, the key question is why he believed that it was important that his readers believe in the picture of unity that he was presenting of "one nation, indivisible." Were we not such a nation, then one might well fear, as spelled out in the early essays in *The Federalist*, that the United States would fragment into two or three separate nations along the Atlantic Coast (with more to come, no doubt, via internal settlement and expansion), with dire consequences of endless war as in Europe. That was obviously the central issue posed in 1861, though in fact the first stirrings of secession came from New England, during the Hartford Convention in 1814, and then again via the call by the great abolitionist William Lloyd Garrison for "No Union with Slaveholders."

The Union was preserved, but at a terrible cost beyond the 750,000 lives lost between 1861 and 1865. "Reconstruction" did not in fact lead to genuine "regime change" in the ostensibly defeated South, which in fact gained additional political representation in the House and the Electoral College because freed slaves were now counted as whole persons (who were successfully, as the twentieth century arrived, denied the right to vote purportedly guaranteed by the Fifteenth Amendment). Race is the never-ending fundamental dividing line in American politics and culture, as W. E. B. DuBois suggested more than a century ago. But, as Madison noted in *Federalist* No. 10, religion, too, was a source of basic division and "factionalization," seen most clearly in the remarkable influence of Christian Evangelicals, who overwhelmingly voted for Donald Trump (and later, in Alabama, for Roy Moore in the Alabama Senate race).

Can we truly be confident that the United States will (or ought to) survive into the indefinite future as a single country? It cannot be plausibly described as a "nation-state," for the very meaning of "multi-nationalism" is that "We the People" are a collection of disparate groups whose differences were submerged by rule by a more or less hegemonic elite of "WASPs," a term that was still in use when I entered graduate school in 1962 and differentiated sharply between

"mainstream" Christianity (which for some Americans still did not include Roman Catholicism, as revealed by the fact that the "P" stood
for Protestants and that JFK in 1960 had to explain to Baptists in
Houston that he would not in fact be a puppet of the Papacy) and the
more exotic, widely ignored or simply discredited, "Fundamentalist"
sects. Indeed, the term "Evangelical Protestant" was scarcely on the
horizon. But that hegemony is long gone, and increasingly I have the
feeling that we as a political culture are, in Matthew Arnold's terms,
"ignorant armies clashing by night." Polling data indicates that a surprising number of Americans, especially under forty, are increasingly
willing to countenance, at least abstractly, the possibility of secession.
The "mystic chords of memory" evoked by Abraham Lincoln in 1861
may not sound so clearly among contemporary generations who are
basically ignorant of American history and, even if at least somewhat
informed, may be more inclined to emphasize the less attractive and
less inspiring aspects of that history.

Today we live in a country of approximately 325 million persons
living east to west from New York to Hawaii and north to south from
Maine to Florida and Texas. As indicated earlier, it would not be surprising if Puerto Rico asked to join the Union in the relatively near
future. One can say with absolute confidence that none of the framers
could have conceived of the reality within which we attempt to achieve
the magnificent goals set out in the Preamble to the Constitution. We
can cite *Federalist* No. 10 for the idea of the "extended republic," but
it requires remarkable confidence to believe in its reality, at least if we
take the idea of republican government very seriously.

A reality of politics around the world is the presence of serious secessionist movements, most dramatically, of course, at least in 2018,
in Catalonia. But one can surely wonder if the United Kingdom will
maintain itself in its present form, given its own secession from the
European Union against the opposition of Scotland; Québec nationalism, though currently in abeyance, might nonetheless revive in the
future to call into question the maintenance of Canada. And these are
only the most obvious examples. Unless one is committed to an ulti-
mate theory of path dependence by which any existing national borders become self-legitimating and impervious to change, then the
question of secession is always available even if it is most often latent.

But Americans have a special problem suppressing the issue because our own independence in 1776 was in fact a secession from the

British Empire rather than a revolutionary attempt to capture control of the central government in London. As we noted in one of our joint essays, borrowing from Harvard historian David Armitage, the most influential part of the Declaration of Independence worldwide has not in fact been the list of "unalienable Rights," but, rather, the assertion that any "one people" can presumably empower itself to throw off what it considers the shackles of illegitimate governance and proclaim their own right of self-government.

So I conclude this exchange by asking you (and, implicitly, our readers) if you (and they) are quite so confident of the continued existence of the present territorial form of the United States of America as they might have been, say, twenty years ago. Is it truly unthinkable that our children and grandchildren will find themselves confronting genuine political movements, led by "respectable" figures, in behalf of "Pacifica," "Cascadia," "New England" (or "Atlantica"), or even "Dixie" or Texas? You tend to present an almost optimistic picture of the American future that will look back on this winter of our discontent as the prelude to a sunnier reality when Trumpism will be exposed as a sham and American politics will right itself. I hope you are correct, of course, but I am less optimistic.

It has been a sheer pleasure engaging in this exchange, save for the fact that it has forced us to confront what are distinctly unpleasant aspects about the country we live in and love.

Sandy

JANUARY 5, 2018

Dear Sandy,

American democracy is suffering from constitutional rot. But constitutional rot is not always fatal, and there are good reasons to think that it will not be fatal in the present case.

The Cycles of Constitutional Change

Mark Twain is supposed to have said that history doesn't repeat itself, but it does rhyme.[1] In the present context, this saying has two meanings. First, we can learn a lot about the future by thinking about the past. Second, much change is not linear, but occurs in cycles or has attributes that wax and wane over time.

There are at least three different cycles at work, and their intersection has generated our present dismal condition.

The first is the cycle of the rise, fall, and birth of political regimes, which I have discussed several times in our correspondence. We are nearing the end of the political regime begun in 1980 with Ronald Reagan's election—the regime in which the conservative movement captured and remade the Republican Party in its own image. That regime is now dying, but a new regime has yet to be born.

1. It is not actually clear that he ever said this, but the quote has stuck to him. The closest example comes from Mark Twain and Charles Dudley Warner, *The Gilded Age* (Harper & Brothers, 1915), 2:178 ("History never repeats itself, but the kaleidoscopic combinations of the pictured present often seem to be constructed out of the broken fragments of antique legends.")

What the new regime will look like is still unclear. The Republicans might gain a second wind, as they did in 1896, when they beat back William Jennings Bryan's populist insurgency and continued their political dominance for thirty more years. In our own day, a transformed Republican Party would probably be a Trumpist regime organized around a combination of American nationalism, conservative Christianity, and bare-knuckled capitalism.

I expect that a Trumpist coalition will win its share of elections around the country—especially in the South—but the odds that it can form a durable new national majority coalition seem longer every day. The more likely candidate for a new political regime will probably be on the left and will probably feature the Democrats as the dominant party. The new coalition will be the natural evolution of the Obama coalition—of minorities, millennials, professionals, suburbanites, and women—but how that coalition negotiates the choice between economic populism and the soft neoliberalism of the Clinton/Obama years is difficult to say. Even so, a durable majority coalition in the United States has to make its peace with capitalism, no matter how much it hopes to tame or reform it.

Transitions between political regimes are often periods of great anxiety and confusion, in which government seems especially dysfunctional. But that transition will be over, I predict, in the next three or four election cycles. For better or for worse, in ten years' time our politics will look very different than it does now—I very much hope for the better. People will stop talking about how dysfunctional our Constitution is, even if they don't like the policies that the new regime enacts.

What makes this particular transition especially difficult, however, is that it overlaps with a second cycle—of political polarization and depolarization. We are near (what I can only hope) is the peak of a cycle of increasing partisan polarization that began in the culture wars that commenced with the 1968 election and accelerated during the 1990s. A key characteristic of the Reagan regime has been ever-increasing party polarization and conflict extension—so that the parties line up on opposite sides of almost every issue.

Extreme polarization makes transition to a new regime especially difficult because defenders of the existing regime have almost nothing in common with the views of the new dominant party. Thus, the political ascension of a new majority coalition seems especially dangerous and threatening, leading defenders of the old order—in this case Republican conservatives—to try everything they can think of to prevent the transition from occurring. As a result, this transition will prove far more difficult and fraught than the transition that produced the New Deal in the 1930s or the Reagan Revolution itself. Both of these transitions occurred in periods of relative depolarization, in which many cross-party agreements were still possible, so that it was possible for the losers to think that they would not lose everything in the transformation.

As if that were not bad enough, there is yet a third cycle at work. This is the cycle of the rise and fall of republican government, organized around the idea of constitutional rot. The idea of rot suggests a one-way ratchet: after all, rotten fruit does not get fresher over time. And certainly the founding generation, influenced by Plato and Polybius, assumed that republics inevitably corrode and turn into tyrannies; they do not rebound.

Yet we must remember that the idea of "rot" is only a metaphor. Even republics that have fallen into corruption can bounce back and rejuvenate themselves. Indeed, the whole point of a well-designed constitution is to offer what I earlier called republican insurance—to minimize the damage from inevitable periods of political corruption and preserve the constitutional system until it can be restored. The history of the United States suggests that our political constitution is resilient; that it can handle a considerable degree of corruption and still reform itself, rather than simply devolve into autocracy or anarchy. This possibility—that the Constitution can be redeemed—generates a cycle of constitutional rot and reform, a cycle in which we have long been descending.

Our current situation arises from the intersection of these three cycles. First, we are near the end of a dying political regime, which produces anxiety, confusion, and the fear that government will forever be dysfunctional. Second, we are approaching the peak of a cycle of political polarization—a period of mutual recrimination and misunderstanding unlike any we have seen since the Civil War. Third, we have descended ever further into a cycle of constitutional rot—as our government has become increasingly oligarchical and our representatives promote the interests of well-paid backers rather than the public good. Indeed, our national politics has not seemed so corrupt since the excesses of the Gilded Age.

Put these three cycles together, and it is no wonder that people despair for American democracy.

The intersection of these three cycles of change is not accidental—
the phenomena are interrelated. The Reagan regime—especially following Newt Gingrich's rise to power—deliberately promoted political polarization and demonization of the opposition in order to make
the Republican Party a majority party and keep it in power. Increasing polarization, in turn, provided ample cover for government policies that increased economic inequality and shifted economic risks
from the wealthy onto the poor and middle class. Polarization and
economic inequality, you may recall, are two of the Four Horsemen
of constitutional rot. Moreover, increasing polarization and economic
inequality—combined with the Reagan-era ideology that government
was the problem and not the solution—exacerbated the public's growing distrust of government and expertise generally. Increasing venality
and incompetence, in turn, generated a series of policy disasters, including the S&L crisis of the late 1980s (made worse by the reigning
ideology of financial deregulation), the Iraq War, and the global financial crisis. Growing incompetence and corruption seemed to justify
the loss of trust. Add all of these factors together, and the result is toxic
for democracy.

The Rhyming of History

Can the United States recover? There are two analogous situations
in American history that combined strong political polarization with
severe constitutional rot. In each case, the country responded to corruption with periods of reform, renewing its commitments to democracy and republicanism. The first example is the period before the
Civil War, which led to Reconstruction; the second is the Gilded Age,
which led to the Progressive Era. That these two periods of rot and
reform follow so closely one after the other should be additional evidence that constitutional rot is not a fatal condition.

Before the Civil War, an oligarchy of slave-owning interests—which
early Republicans called the Slave Power—dominated American politics. Wealthy plantation owners and their political allies directed government policy in the interests of a slave economy—the economic
exploitation of ownership of human beings—at the expense of small
farmers and tradespeople. By the late Jacksonian period, the Slave

Power had become especially ruthless in its drive for self-preservation and aggrandizement. As the regime ended, defenders of slavery, fearing that they could no longer dominate the national government, rebelled.

In the Gilded Age, America was increasingly dominated by a capitalist oligarchy of businessmen whose enormous fortunes had been created by the expansion of railroads and the growth of industrial capitalism. These were the oligarchs whom Teddy Roosevelt famously called the "malefactors of great wealth." They and their political servants seized hold of the early nineteenth-century ideology of free labor, equality, freedom, and progress, and twisted it into a defense of wealth and privilege in what Clinton Rossiter called "the Great Intellectual Train Robbery of American History."[2]

Both the close of the Jacksonian era and the Gilded Age were also periods in which the dominant political regime became exhausted and ripe for overthrow by a new political party. It happened in one case, but not in the other. Jacksonian democracy, corrupted by the Slave Power, gave way to a new regime dominated by the anti-slavery Republicans. American democracy was rejuvenated, and the country experienced what Abraham Lincoln called "a new birth of freedom," but at the cost of three-quarters of a million lives. The transformative years of Reconstruction, however, quickly led to the financial and political corruption of the Gilded Age. In the 1890s, the Democrats and populists tried to create a new political regime responsive to the problems of industrial capitalism. They failed, in part because the incumbent Democratic president, Grover Cleveland, was an economic conservative who also had the misfortune to be president during the Panic of 1893. A Democratic insurgent, William Jennings Bryan, proved unable to forge a successful alliance of populists and Democrats. As a result, Republicans regrouped and created a new coalition around a new set of issues that allowed them to continue their political dominance until the 1930s. Although the populists were defeated, these years launched a period of Progressive reform in both parties, which, in turn, eventually led to the further reforms of the New Deal.

Which situation is most like ours? Given your focus on the danger of secession, Sandy, you might be tempted to pick the two decades leading up to the Civil War. I disagree. For reasons I explained

2. Clinton L. Rossiter, *Conservatism in America* (Knopf, 1962), 128.

in my letter of November 1, 2015 (how long ago that seems!), there is no chance of a successful secessionist movement in the United States in the near future. Obviously at some point the United States will fall apart, as virtually every dominant power has in world history. But we are nowhere near that point. And, for geostrategic reasons, there is little chance that the United States would allow a division into hypothetical Red and Blue Americas sharing a long, common border that would be impossible to police or secure. The problem would be even worse if both countries are armed with nuclear weapons, and one tilts toward Russia while the other tilts toward the European Union. Secession is a fantasy (or a fear, depending on one's perspective) that distracts us from the hard work of rebuilding American democracy.

The better analogy, I think, is to the last years of the Gilded Age—or, rather, the First Gilded Age, since it now seems clear that we are living in a Second Gilded Age, in which the Koch brothers, financial Masters of the Universe, and the leaders of technology companies play the structural roles of the Carnegies, Vanderbilts, and Rockefellers. The United States was as divided and diverse at the end of the nineteenth century as it is today. There were the same concerns that our Constitution was outmoded and that we were too internally differentiated to survive as a nation. And yet we did survive, and, if anything, the waves of immigration strengthened the country in the decades ahead. The same, I think, will prove true today.

America suffered serious constitutional rot in the Gilded Age, a period that has many similarities to our own. Technological progress had created vast new fortunes and huge corporations (then called trusts) that were unlike anything Americans had seen before. The country had experienced (and would continue to experience) waves of immigrants from many different places, whose presence generated increasing resentment from existing populations. These complaints about immigrants sound familiar today: The newcomers did not speak English or spoke it badly; they did not assimilate; they were dangerous, criminal, and politically radical. Their religious views were suspect. They did not understand the genius of Anglo-American constitutionalism, and they would destroy America's greatness.

Racial antagonisms also grew: The Republican Party finally tired of attempting to protect black civil rights and acquiesced in the Democrats' racist one-party system of governance in the South. Jim Crow emerged, and strategies of black disenfranchisement accelerated in the last years of the nineteenth century and the first years of the twentieth.

At both the state and federal levels, the conduct of government was increasingly corrupt and controlled by a small group of powerful economic interests, who shamelessly used state power to enrich themselves. Indeed, during the Gilded Age, government was more or less for sale, exacerbating already-growing inequalities of wealth. It was a time of increasing social unrest, and many people gave up on the political system entirely, turning to violence, rioting, and dreams of radical revolution.

But this period of constitutional rot was also the beginning of great political change. Public outcry at inequality and corruption led to the populist and progressive movements. Public activism generated successive waves of experimentation and legislation in the federal government and especially in the states—including four federal constitutional amendments. As the nineteenth century drew to a close, one might well have feared that American democracy was morally bankrupt and that our experiment in republican government was on a downhill slide from which it would never recover. Yet the United States survived this cycle of constitutional rot and came out of it even stronger.

We are now in the middle of our Second Gilded Age—a period of increasing financial and political corruption, economic inequality, racial animosity, and anxieties over immigration and globalization. Government is once again for sale. The public lacks trust in government because government has repeatedly proved itself untrustworthy. Our national leaders are hardly better than those of the late nineteenth century. Instead of the "honest president" and economic conservative Grover Cleveland, we have had the upright and neoliberal Barack Obama. Instead of the "human iceberg" Benjamin Harrison and the business-friendly imperialist William McKinley, we have had the foolhardy George W. Bush and now have the dangerously ignorant, racist, and corrupt Donald Trump. The next Teddy Roosevelt—much less the next Franklin—has yet to appear on the scene.

Perhaps history will not repeat itself, but I am fairly confident that it will rhyme. I predict that Americans will tire of incompetence and venality. They will cry out for a government they can once again trust. And they will mobilize to achieve that goal. The coming decades will produce a renaissance of political reforms, especially at the state and local level, but at the federal level as well. I also predict a period of constitutional creativity. Most of the reforms will occur outside of Article V, for reasons I've described earlier in our exchange. But, as in the Progressive Era, we may have a few Article V amendments as well. And at the state level, I predict an explosion of constitutional experimentation.

For that to happen, however, our current politics will have to change. This is somewhat easier at the state level, precisely because states have more avenues for political and constitutional reform than the federal government. At the federal level, there are two ways that reform will occur.

The most straightforward is that one of the two major political parties, probably the Democrats, becomes the dominant party in a new regime, and its policy goals mesh with constitutional and political reform. That is the story of the First Reconstruction led by Republicans following the Civil War. (If this happened, our current situation would differ from the close of the Gilded Age, when the Democrats tried and failed to establish a new regime.) Mark Graber has argued that serious constitutional reforms usually require one party to become dominant, at which point it attempts to alter the constitutional order to entrench its constitutional vision. As Graber notes, following the Civil War, the ascendant Republicans, who regarded themselves as the loyal party of Union, designed the Reconstruction Amendments and made many other institutional changes—including the creation of the Justice Department and the expansion of federal judicial power— to keep the government in the hands of Union loyalists and to promote their values and their vision of democracy.

A second possibility is a bipartisan (or multi-party) movement for constitutional reform. There are two central examples: The first occurred during the Progressive Era in reaction to the corruption of the Gilded Age. Although the Republican Party still dominated national politics, progressive or reformist wings emerged in both parties—in addition to various minor parties. This led to a rich period of constitutional experimentation and reform: four Article V amendments, the creation of the Federal Reserve to remove monetary policy from everyday political struggle, antitrust laws to reduce corporate power, bans on corporate contributions, extension of suffrage to women, educational reforms, the development of initiative and referendum in state governments, and administrative and good-government reforms in cities.

Another example of a bipartisan movement for constitutional reform occurred in the civil rights era that began with the direct-action phase of the civil rights movement and *Brown v. Board of Education*. Although the New Deal Democrats remained dominant, their party was increasingly fractured between its (mostly) northern liberal and southern conservative wings. That division led the liberal wing to join forces with liberal and moderate Republicans. This was the era of the great civil rights acts—including the Voting Rights Act of 1965—the expansion of free speech rights, the abolition of the poll tax, and the Warren Court's reapportionment decisions.

I expect that our current bitter polarization will prevent a bipartisan approach to constitutional reform, and that only the first paradigm—constitutional reform led by a single dominant party—will succeed. After all, the bipartisan reforms of the civil rights era occurred during a period of depolarization between the two major political parties. If anything, these reforms, especially the Voting Rights Act, led to the repolarization of the parties, as southern whites increasingly shifted their political allegiance to the Republican Party. Donald Trump's presidency is the outcome of the Republican Party's extended flirtation with white racial resentment.

On the other hand, the reforms of the Progressive Era began during a period in which polarization was still quite robust. Americans who were still quite divided along party lines were nevertheless able to rid the nation of a very pronounced case of constitutional rot. These reforms occurred alongside gradual depolarization. In fact, this period of constitutional reform may have even helped enhance depolarization.

A Reform Agenda for a New Regime

If I am right that we are on the cusp of a period of constitutional creativity, what kinds of reforms should we hope for? To explain and defend them all would require another book. Instead, I will simply list eight reforms that might help renew our constitutional order. Each of them assumes a change in our politics along the lines described above—that we will someday have a new dominant coalition, or that we will experience a second Progressive Era. Many of these changes can occur at the state level, and most do not require an Article V amendment.

(1) First and foremost, Americans must reform their voting sys-

tems. You have already noted that we could replace the statutory requirement of single-member House districts with an at-large system of proportional voting. This reform would make many House races newly competitive; and it would give greater opportunities for moderate as well as strongly ideological candidates.

(2) The Supreme Court may eventually hold certain kinds of gerrymandering unconstitutional.[3] Whether or not it does so, individual states can and should shift to nonpartisan state electoral commissions to draw district boundaries and manage elections generally.

(3) States can expand voting times and polling places and make it easier for more Americans to vote. States can adopt automatic registration when people obtain or renew their driver's licenses or other identifying documents. If states think that voter identification is important, they should make voter identification easy and inexpensive to obtain, rather than using it as a device to restrict the right to vote. The federal government should renew the Voting Rights Act to deal with the endlessly creative ways that politicians attempt to rig the electoral system. This last reform, unfortunately, may require not only a new political regime, but a saner Supreme Court than the myopic majority that crippled the Voting Rights Act in *Shelby County v. Holder*.[4]

(4) Serious campaign finance reform also awaits a friendlier Supreme Court. But when that occurs, both the states and the federal government have many options. This is not the place to offer an extended list, so I will mention only two. Disclosure requirements that would reveal which wealthy donors are contributing to super PACs are already constitutional. An even more important reform is to tighten restrictions on coordination between super PACs and candidates. The 2016 election was especially farcical in this respect. It was an open secret that coordination was rampant; the press casually spoke of the candidates' super PACs even though this implied illegal coordination. It might also be a good idea to reconstitute the Federal Election Commission as a nonpartisan rather than a bipartisan entity, so that it finally becomes serious about enforcing the federal campaign laws.

(5) There are several ways to reform the Electoral College without a constitutional amendment. One is the Fair Vote state compact men-

---

3. It was twice presented with the opportunity in 2018 in *Gill v. Whitford*, 585 U.S. __ (2018) and *Benisek v. Lamone*, 585 U.S. __ (2018), but each time refused to reach the merits.

4. 570 U.S. 529 (2013).

tioned earlier.[5] It requires cooperation by states with a majority of electoral votes and possibly congressional ratification. Ned Foley has offered a different fix that each state can perform on its own.[6] States can implement instant runoffs in presidential elections: Voters rank their preferences among multiple candidates; in counting the votes, the state eliminates the candidate with the lowest vote total. It transfers these votes to the voters' second choice. It continues this process until one candidate has an absolute majority. Adopting an instant runoff system would prevent third-party candidates like Jill Stein or Ralph Nader from swinging the election to a candidate who fails to win even a plurality, like Donald Trump or George W. Bush. An instant runoff system might even encourage more third-party candidates, because voters could support them secure in the knowledge that doing so would not swing the election to an especially disfavored candidate. For this reason, states may want to adopt an instant runoff system for many different offices, not just for the U.S. presidency.

(6) Enforcement of antitrust and pro-competition laws was lax during much of the Reagan regime. Both the federal and state governments should resume serious enforcement, not simply to protect consumer welfare—the standard neoliberal justification—but for larger reasons of political economy. The concentration of economic power in a small number of private entities has baleful effects on democracy. It is an important factor in the creation and maintenance of oligarchy. The problem of the First Gilded Age was not that it reduced consumer welfare; it was that powerful trusts leveraged their control of the economy to dominate politics at the expense of the public interest. The same thing is happening today; we need a new age of antitrust enforcement and new laws and doctrines to combat new threats to democracy.

Shifting the focus of antitrust laws from consumer welfare to democracy is especially important because the greatest danger of the new digital titans of commerce like Facebook and Google is not that they will charge consumers too much. Instead, these businesses offer their

5. Fair Vote, http://www.fairvote.org/national_popular_vote#endorsers_of_the_npv_plan.

6. Edward B. Foley, "How States Can Fix the Electoral College and Prevent Future Trumps," *USA Today*, November 9, 2017, https://www.usatoday.com/story/opinion/2017/11/09/fix-electoral-college-prevent-future-trumps-adopt-runoff-voting-edward-foley-column/839492001/.

services for free in exchange for ever more personal data about end users. Facebook uses algorithms to personalize content in order to monopolize the attention of individual consumers. This business model not only helped exacerbate our divisive political culture; it also made it possible for foreign and domestic malefactors to hijack Facebook's system to disseminate fake news and propaganda. Serious antitrust enforcement might have prevented Facebook from buying up promising competitors before they had a chance to challenge its hegemony over social media. In turn, a digital ecology with multiple Facebooks instead of one might have been less vulnerable to foreign manipulation.

(7) Both you and I have supported eighteen-year terms for justices of the Supreme Court, which would guarantee a presidential appointment every two years. One example of how this could be accomplished is a 2009 proposal offered by a group of thirty-three legal academics, former state court judges, and practitioners, and headed by Duke University's Paul Carrington.[7] That proposal preserves life tenure but defines the quorum for hearing Supreme Court cases as the nine justices most junior in service. More senior justices who have not retired will join the quorum in cases of death, disability, or recusal by justices in the quorum. Senior justices may also participate in the selection of cases to be heard by the quorum, and they may sit by designation in the lower federal courts. This proposal is consistent with Article III's requirement that judges shall hold their offices during good behavior, and therefore can be achieved by an Act of Congress.

(8) One can only hope that the corruption of the Trump presidency will generate a wide range of reforms of the executive branch, including laws to prevent financial conflicts of interest and mandatory disclosure of tax returns for all presidential candidates. Conservatives have been arguing for reform of the administrative state for some time, and although I do not agree with this critique in all respects, much reform can occur through modest changes in judicial doctrine. Whether you find it ironic or not, it is possible that Trump-appointed conservative

---

7. On the Carrington proposal, see Jack M. Balkin, "Reforming the Supreme Court," *Balkinization*, February 13, 2009, https://balkin.blogspot.com/2009/02/reforming-supreme-court.html. For a demonstration of how the proposal would work in practice, see Jack M. Balkin, "The Rotation of the Justices: A Thought Experiment," *Balkinization*, May 20, 2009, https://balkin.blogspot.com/2009/05/rotation-of-justices-thought-experiment.html.

judges and justices will lead the way in making executive power more accountable in the administrative state. Reform of presidential war-making powers is probably the hardest nut to crack. But the first place to start, it seems to me, is to repeal the 2001 Authorization for Use of Military Force and replace it with a narrower grant. Above all, I think that some form of a congressional vote of no confidence, as described in my last letter, will help restrain executive overreach in many areas at once. That, however, does require an Article V amendment.

* * *

Some may think this list of future constitutional reforms is too timid; others may think it too bold, or even foolhardy. Some may think I have left out the most important problems; others may think I have not offered the right solutions to the problems I do identify. This is only a preliminary account, and I welcome suggestions for improvement. But the most important point, it seems to me, is that we should see the glint of opportunity in our current darkness; and recognize that the cycles of change will soon open doors that now seem forever locked.

We began our letters two years ago discussing the general problems of dysfunction in the American constitutional system. Suddenly those problems crystallized in Trump's ascension to power. I do not profess to know how Trump's presidency will end. But I believe that Trump's greatest gift to the country is the gift of destruction—not of the country, but of the coalition he leads and the complacent oligarchy that strangles our democracy.

The greatest irony of a fool like Trump is that by betraying his working-class base and wrecking his party, he may well help make American democracy great again. He is the unwitting agent of reform. Even as we despair of our current situation, we must recognize how, from the smoldering wreckage of his presidency, something valuable might yet be built. Out of disaster comes hope, out of hope comes renewal; we must have the faith to believe in the possibilities and see them through.

Your devoted friend,
Jack

ACKNOWLEDGMENTS

This book began with an April 2014 invitation to Jack from Mark Rosen and David Orentlicher to give a keynote address at a symposium entitled "Partisan Conflict, Political Structure, and Culture." As soon as Jack had been reeled in by these blandishments, Mark and David then engaged in the traditional academic bait-and-switch, changing the location and timing of the conference and Jack's role in it several times. Finally, however, Mark and David secured a home for the event. They also hit upon the brilliant idea of arranging a debate between Jack and Sandy on constitutional dysfunction, and thus the idea for this book was born.

We thank not only Mark and David for their persistence in making the conference come about, but also the wonderful students at the Indiana University Robert H. McKinney School of Law and the *Indiana Law Review* for hosting the event and publishing the resulting exchange. We would also like to thank the participants at a faculty workshop at Yale Law School, where portions of this book were presented.

We are also deeply indebted to our editor at the University of Chicago Press, Chuck Myers, for his support of this project as we sought to turn our epistolary exchanges into a book.

Special thanks go to two individuals. The first is Mark Graber, who has been a constant interlocutor in our discussions about constitutional dysfunction—as well as a beloved friend. He has influenced our views on constitutional history, on constitutional change, and on constitutional design in countless ways. The second is Stephen Griffin, a friend of many years and one of the country's most thoughtful scholars on constitutional change and war powers, who has taught us much about the role of trust in political constitutions. This book is dedicated to them.

Our greatest thanks, however, go to our spouses, Cynthia Levinson and Margaret Wolfe. They have, quite unselfishly, given us their love, support, and encouragement, when either our creative process—or our procrastination—made us less than ideal companions.

* * *

Several of the letters in this book—or parts of them—have also appeared in a number of blog posts and essays, as well as in our *Indiana Law Review* exchange. We
have revised, edited, and recombined this material for this book. The revised and
edited portions of the following blog posts, essays, and articles appear with permission of the respective copyright holders:

Sanford Levinson and Jack M. Balkin, "Democracy and Dysfunction: An
   Exchange," *Indiana Law Review* 50 (2016): 281.
Jack M. Balkin, "Constitutional Crisis and Constitutional Rot," *Maryland Law
   Review* 77, no. 1 (2017): 147. This essay also appears in *Constitutional Democ-
   racy in Crisis?*, ed. Mark A. Graber, Sanford Levinson, and Mark Tushnet
   (Oxford University Press, 2018).
Jack M. Balkin, "Constitutional Rot," in *Can It Happen Here? Authoritarianism
   in America*, ed. Cass R. Sunstein (Dey Street Books, 2018).
Jack M. Balkin, "How to Tell If You Are in a Constitutional Crisis," *Balkinization*,
   February 7, 2017, https://balkin.blogspot.com/2017/02/how-to-tell-if-you
   -are-in.html.
Jack Balkin, "Obama Hoped to Be a Transformational President. He Failed," *Vox*,
   January 19, 2017, https://www.vox.com/the-big-idea/2017/1/19/14323552
   /obama-legacy-reagan-clinton-conservative-liberal.
Jack M. Balkin, "Scenes from a Disjunctive Presidency," *Balkinization*, August 29,
   2017, https://balkin.blogspot.com/2017/08/scenes-from-disjunctive-presi
   dency.html.
Jack M. Balkin, "The Tax Bill and Constitutional Rot," *Balkinization*, December
   21, 2017, https://balkin.blogspot.com/2017/12/the-tax-bill-and-constitutional
   -rot.html.
Jack M. Balkin, "Trumping the Constitution," *Balkinization*, June 14, 2017,
   https://balkin.blogspot.com/2017/06/trumping-constitution.html.

BIBLIOGRAPHY

Ackerman, Bruce. *We the People: Foundations.* Vol. 1. Belknap Press of Harvard University Press, 1991.

Albert, Richard. "The Fusion of Presidentialism and Parliamentarism." *American Journal of Comparative Law* 57 (2009): 531–77.

Amar, Akhil Reed. *America's Unwritten Constitution: The Precedents and Principles We Live By.* Random House, 2012.

Amar, Vikram David. "Response: The Case for Reforming Presidential Elections by Subconstitutional Means: The Electoral College, the National Popular Vote Compact, and Congressional Power." *Georgetown Law Journal* 100 (2011): 237.

Azari, Julia. "Trump's Presidency Signals the End of the Reagan Era." *Vox,* December 1, 2016. https://www.vox.com/mischiefs-of-faction/2016/12/1/13794680/trump-presidency-reagan-era-end.

Balkin, Jack M. "Constitutional Hardball and Constitutional Crises." *Quinnipiac Law Review* 26 (2008): 579.

———. *Constitutional Redemption: Political Faith in an Unjust World.* Harvard University Press, 2011.

———. "The Framework Model and Constitutional Interpretation." In *Philosophical Foundations of Constitutional Law*, edited by David Dyzenhaus and Malcom Thorburn. Oxford University Press, 2016.

———. "The Last Days of Disco: Why the American Political System Is Dysfunctional." *Boston University Law Review* 94 (2014): 1159.

———. *Living Originalism.* Belknap Press of Harvard University Press, 2011.

———. "Obama Hoped to Be a Transformational President. He Failed." *Vox,* January 19, 2017. https://www.vox.com/the-big-idea/2017/1/19/14323552/obama-legacy-reagan-clinton-conservative-liberal.

———. "Reforming the Supreme Court." *Balkinization,* February 13, 2009. https://balkin.blogspot.com/2009/02/reforming-supreme-court.html.

———. "Republicanism and the Constitution of Opportunity." *Texas Law Review* 94 (2016): 1427.

———. "The Rotation of the Justices: A Thought Experiment." *Balkinization*, May 20, 2009. https://balkin.blogspot.com/2009/05/rotation-of-justices -thought-experiment.html.

———. "What Kind of President Will Donald Trump Become, Part I." *Balkinization*, November 13, 2016. https://balkin.blogspot.com/2016/11/what-kind-of -president-will-trump_13.html.

———. "What Kind of President Will Donald Trump Become, Part II—Donald Trump and the Politics of Disjunction." *Balkinization*, November 14, 2016. https://balkin.blogspot.com/2016/11/what-kind-of-president-will-trump .html [https://perma.cc/8U52-WP59].

———. "Which Republican Constitution?" *Constitutional Commentary* 32 (2017): 31.

Black, Charles L., Jr. *Impeachment: A Handbook.* Yale University Press, 1998.

Branham, J. Alexander, Stuart N. Soroka, and Christopher Wlezien. "When Do the Rich Win?" *Political Science Quarterly* 132 (2017): 43–62.

Brecht, Bertolt. "To Those Who Follow in Our Wake." Translated by Scott Horton. *Harper's* blog. http://harpers.org/blog/2008/01/brecht-to-those -who-follow-in-our-wake/.

Brownstein, Ronald. "The New Political Math." *RealClearPolitics*, August 24, 2012. http://www.realclearpolitics.com/2012/08/23/the_new_political _math_288266.html [https://perma.cc/Y977-V8DB].

Bueno de Mesquita, Bruce, and Alastair Smith. *The Dictator's Handbook: Why Bad Behavior Is Almost Always Good Politics.* Public Affairs, 2012.

Bulman-Pozen, Jessica, and Heather K. Gerken. "Uncooperative Federalism." *Yale Law Journal* 118, no. 7 (2009): 1256.

Cooper, Charles J. "Confronting the Administrative State." *National Affairs*, no. 26 (Summer 2018). http://www.nationalaffairs.com/publications/detail /confronting-the-administrative-state [https://perma.cc/XH7A-C6TE].

Dahl, Robert A. *How Democratic Is the United States Constitution?* Yale University Press, 2002.

———. *Pluralist Democracy in the United States: Conflict and Consent.* Rand McNally, 1968.

———. *A Preface to Democratic Theory.* University of Chicago Press, 1956.

Edsall, Mary D., and Thomas Byrne Edsall. *Chain Reaction: The Impact of Race, Rights, and Taxes on American Politics.* Norton, 1992.

Ellis, Richard J. *The Development of the American Presidency.* Routledge, 2012.

Enns, Peter K. "Relative Policy Support and Coincidental Representation." *Perspectives on Politics* 13 (2015): 1053–64.

Eskridge, William N., Jr., and John Ferejohn. "Super-Statutes." *Duke Law Journal* 50 (2001): 1215.

Ezrow, Natasha M., and Erica Frantz. *Dictators and Dictatorships: Understanding Authoritarian Regimes and Their Leaders.* Continuum, 2011.

Fair Vote. "National Popular Vote." http://www.fairvote.org/national_popular _vote#endorsers_of_the_npv_plan.

Finn, John E. *Peopling the Constitution*. University Press of Kansas, 2014.

Foley, Edward B. "How States Can Fix the Electoral College and Prevent Future Trumps." *USA Today*, November 9, 2017. https://www.usatoday.com/story /opinion/2017/11/09/fix-electoral-college-prevent-future-trumps-adopt -runoff-voting-edward-foley-column/839492001/.

Ford, Henry Jones. *The Rise and Growth of American Politics*. Macmillan, 1898.

Gallie, W. B. "Essentially Contested Concepts." *Proceedings of the Aristotelian Society* 56, no. 1 (June 1, 1956): 167–98.

Gerhardt, Michael J. *Impeachment: What Everyone Needs to Know*. Oxford University Press, 2018.

Gerken, Heather K. "Dissenting by Deciding." *Stanford Law Review* 57 (2005): 1745.

Gilens, Martin, and Benjamin I. Page. "Testing Theories of American Politics: Elites, Interest Groups, and Average Citizens." *Perspectives on Politics* 12 (2014): 561–81.

Ginsburg, Tom, and Aziz Huq. *How to Save a Constitutional Democracy*. University of Chicago Press, 2018.

Graber, Mark A. "Belling the Partisan Cats: Preliminary Thoughts on Identifying and Mending a Dysfunctional Constitutional Order." *Boston University Law Review* 94 (2014): 611.

———. "Constructing Constitutional Politics: Thaddeus Stevens, John Bingham, and the Forgotten Fourteenth Amendment." August 19, 2014, SSRN. https:// papers.ssrn.com/sol3/papers.cfm?abstract_id=2483355.

———. "The Countermajoritarian Difficulty: From Courts to Congress to Constitutional Order." *Annual Review of Law and Social Science* 4 (2008): 361.

Greve, Michael S. "Yoo to Conservatives: Reverse Course." *Law and Liberty*, September 9, 2013. http://www.libertylawsite.org/2013/09/09/yoo-to-conserva tives-reverse-course/ [https://perma.cc/7LUA-XDPF].

Griffin, Stephen M. *Broken Trust: Dysfunctional Government and Constitutional Reform*. University Press of Kansas, 2015.

———. *Long Wars and the Constitution*. Harvard University Press, 2013.

Huber, John D. "The Vote of Confidence in Parliamentary Democracies." *American Political Science Review* 90 (1996): 269.

Isaacson, Walter. *Benjamin Franklin: An American Life*. Simon & Schuster, 2003.

Kaminsky, Elijah Ben-Zion. "On the Comparison of Presidential and Parliamentary Governments." *Presidential Studies Quarterly* 27 (1997): 221.

Kammen, Michael G. *A Machine That Would Go of Itself: The Constitution in American Culture*. Transaction Publishers, 1986.

Katznelson, Ira. "Anxieties of Democracy." *Boston Review*, September 8, 2015. http://bostonreview.net/forum/ira-katznelson-anxieties-democracy [https:// perma.cc/8EY2-7TXU].

Keck, Thomas M. "Is President Trump More Like Viktor Orbán or Franklin Pierce?" SSRN. February 28, 2018. https://papers.ssrn.com/sol3/papers .cfm?abstract_id=2950015.

Kreitner, Richard. "What Time Is It? Here's What the 2016 Election Tells Us about Obama, Trump, and What Comes Next." *The Nation*, November 22, 2016. https://www.thenation.com/article/what-time-is-it-heres-what-the-2016-election-tells-us-about-obama-trump-and-what-comes-next/.

Layman, Geffrey C., and Thomas M. Carsey. "Party Polarization and 'Conflict Extension' in the American Electorate." *American Journal of Political Science* 46 (2002): 786.

Lemieux, Scott. "Is Donald Trump the Next Jimmy Carter?" *The New Republic*, January 23, 2017. https://newrepublic.com/article/140041/donald-trump-next-jimmy-carter.

Levinson, Daryl J., and Richard H. Pildes. "Separation of Parties, Not Powers." *Harvard Law Review* 119 (2006): 2311.

Levinson, Sanford. *An Argument Open to All: Reading* The Federalist *in the 21st Century*. Yale University Press, 2015.

———. "The 'Dysfunctional Constitution' Thesis." *Connecticut Law Review* 43 (2011): 987.

———. *Framed: America's 51 Constitutions and the Crisis of Governance*. Oxford University Press, 2012.

———. "How the United States Constitution Contributes to the Democratic Deficit in America." *Drake Law Review* 55 (2007): 859.

———. *Our Undemocratic Constitution: Where the Constitution Goes Wrong (and How We the People Can Correct It)*. Oxford University Press, 2006.

———. "The United States and Political Dysfunction: 'What Are Elections For?'" *Drake Law Review* 61 (2012): 959.

———. "What Are We to Do about Dysfunction? Reflections on Structural Constitutional Change and the Irrelevance of Clever Lawyering." *Boston University Law Review* 94 (2014): 1127.

Levinson, Sanford, and Jack M. Balkin. "Constitutional Crises." *University of Pennsylvania Law Review* 157 (2009): 707–53.

———. "Constitutional Dictatorship: Its Dangers and Its Design." *Minnesota Law Review* 94 (2010): 1789866.

Levitsky, Steven, and Daniel Ziblatt. *How Democracies Die*. Crown, 2018.

Madison, James, Alexander Hamilton, and John Jay. *The Federalist Papers*. Edited by Isaac Kramnick. Penguin, 1987.

Mann, Thomas E., and Norman J. Ornstein. *It's Even Worse than It Looks: How the American Constitutional System Collided with the New Politics of Extremism*. Basic Books, 2012.

Matthews, Dylan. "The GOP Health Bill Is a $600 Billion Tax Cut—Almost Entirely for the Wealthy." *Vox*, March 7, 2017. https://www.vox.com/policy-and-politics/2017/3/7/14844362/ahca-ryancare-trumpcare-tax-cut-rich.

Mayhew, David R. "Is Congress 'the Broken Branch'?" *Boston University Law Review* 89 (2009): 357.

———. *Partisan Balance: Why Political Parties Don't Kill the U.S. Constitutional System*. Princeton University Press, 2011.

McCarty, Nolan, Keith T. Poole, and Howard Rosenthal. *Polarized America: The Dance of Ideology and Unequal Riches.* 2nd ed. MIT Press, 2016.

Metzger, Gillian E. "Agencies, Polarization, and the States." *Columbia Law Review* 115 (2015): 1739, 1752–54.

Neubauer, Michael G., and Joel Zeitlin. "Outcomes of Presidential Elections and the House Size." *PS: Political Science and Politics* 36 (2003): 721.

Owens, Caitlin. "Senate GOP Won't Release Draft Health Care Bill." *Axios*, June 12, 2017. https://www.axios.com/senate-gop-wrapping-up-health-care-bill-but-wont-release-it-2440345281.html.

Page, Benjamin I., and Martin Gilens. *Democracy in America? What Has Gone Wrong and What We Can Do about It.* University of Chicago Press, 2017.

Pettit, Philip. *Republicanism: A Theory of Freedom and Government.* Oxford University Press, 1997.

Pocock, J. G. A. *The Machiavellian Moment: Florentine Political Thought and the Atlantic Republican Tradition.* Princeton University Press, 1975.

Posner, Eric, and Adrian Vermeule. *The Executive Unbound: After the Madisonian Republic.* Oxford University Press, 2011.

The Records of the Federal Convention of 1787. Rev. ed. Edited by Max Farrand. Yale University Press, 1966.

Robin, Corey. "The Politics Trump Makes." *n+1*, January 11, 2017. https://nplusonemag.com/online-only/online-only/the-politics-trump-makes/.

Rossiter, Clinton L. *Conservatism in America.* Knopf, 1962.

———. *Constitutional Dictatorship: Crisis Government in the Modern Democracies.* Princeton University Press, 1948.

Roosevelt, Theodore. "Address of President Roosevelt on the Occasion of the Laying of the Corner Stone of the Pilgrim Memorial Monument, Provincetown, MA." August 20, 1907. Government Printing Office, 1907.

Rosenblum, Nancy L. *On the Side of the Angels: An Appreciation of Parties and Partisanship.* Princeton University Press, 2010.

Schmidt, Christopher W. "The Tea Party and the Constitution." *Hastings Constitutional Law Quarterly* 39 (2011): 193.

Schmitt, Carl. *The Concept of the Political.* Translated by George Schwab. University of Chicago Press, 1996.

———. *The Crisis of Parliamentary Democracy.* Translated by Ellen Kennedy. MIT Press, 1998.

Sitaraman, Ganesh. *The Crisis of the Middle-Class Constitution: Why Economic Inequality Threatens Our Republic.* Knopf, 2017.

Skowronek, Stephen. *The Politics Presidents Make: Leadership from John Adams to Bill Clinton.* 1993; reprint, Harvard University Press, 2000.

———. *Presidential Leadership in Political Time: Reprise and Reappraisal.* 2nd ed. University Press of Kansas, 2011.

———. "Twentieth-Century Remedies." *Boston University Law Review* 94 (2014): 795.

Stanley, Jason. *How Propaganda Works.* Princeton University Press, 2016.

Sunstein, Cass R., ed. *Can It Happen Here? Authoritarianism in America.* Harper-Collins, 2018.

———. *Impeachment: A Citizen's Guide.* Harvard University Press, 2018.

Teachout, Zephyr. "The Anti-Corruption Principle." *Cornell Law Review* 94 (2009): 341.

Tribe, Lawrence, and Joshua Matz. *To End a Presidency: The Power of Impeachment.* Basic Books, 2018.

Tulis, Jeffrey K. *The Rhetorical Presidency.* Princeton University Press, 1987.

Tushnet, Mark. "Constitutional Hardball." *John Marshall Law Review* 37 (2004): 523.

Twain, Mark, and Charles Dudley Warner. *The Gilded Age.* Vol. 2. Harper & Brothers, 1915.

Vermeule, Adrian. *Law's Abnegation: From Law's Empire to the Administrative State.* Harvard University Press, 2016.

Voorheis, John, Nolan McCarty, and Boris Shor. "Unequal Incomes, Ideology and Gridlock: How Rising Inequality Increases Political Polarization." August 31, 2015. https://www.princeton.edu/csdp/events/McCarty10012015/McCarty-10012015.pdf.

Weber, Max. "Parliament and Government in Germany Under a New Political Order." In *Weber: Political Writings.* Edited by Peter Lassman and Ronald Spiers. Cambridge University Press, 1994.

Wood, Gordon S. *The Creation of the American Republic, 1776–1787.* University of North Carolina Press, 1969.

Yoo, John. "A Thousand Little Tyrants—Obama's Problems Are a Chance to Rein in the Bureaucracy." *National Review*, September 16, 2013. https://www.nationalreview.com/nrd/articles/357088/thousand-little-tyrants [https://perma.cc/Y7NR-LNG9].

INDEX

Lightning Source UK Ltd.
Milton Keynes UK
UKHW021353190719
346440UK00006B/16/P

9 780226 612041